"WHAT'D I DO, TO BE SO BLACK AND BLUE?"

The blues belongs to black Americans. It is peculiarly black, and peculiarly American. It is the song of people who have been hurt in a particularly elaborate set of ways.

Musician and musicologist Samuel Charters knows, loves, and understands the blues—its rhythms, its feelings, its honesty, its brutality. In THE POETRY OF THE BLUES, he considers the blues and the men and women who have given it to us.

SAMUEL CHARTERS

THE POETRY OF THE BLUES

WITH PHOTOGRAPHS
BY ANN CHARTERS.

AVON
PUBLISHERS OF
DISCUS • CAMELOT • BARD

AVON BOOKS
A division of
The Hearst Corporation
959 Eighth Avenue
New York, New York 10019

First Avon Printing, July, 1970

For Frederick Usher Jr.

When I think of friendship I remember
paths we've walked together by the sea,
at the narrowing of the spit of sand,
the crusted rocks thrusting toward the spray,
our steps so mingled I couldn't tell
the print of your foot from mine.

A NOTE ON SOURCES

The work songs from which much of the blues has been derived were like seeds scattered across the southern landscape. Wherever they strayed the blues sprang up after them and as a man sang the blues he scattered the material farther, until the blues became a nearly communal expression of the Negro in America. Most of the verses of the blues are used by every singer, and they have become the root language for the more personal singers like John Estes and Robert Johnson. I have not mentioned a particular singer as the source for these verses, since this would tend to imply that there is someone who could be thought of as having written them. The best singers, however, often developed a group of verses which became their personal material, and if the verse seemed to be related to one singer I have mentioned his name. Often the verses are used in two or three blues; since the blues is a pliant idiom, so I have not used a title with the verse. I have tried to suggest some of the casualness of blues composition by following the singers' own use of the verse. In those blues which have become a personal poetry I have generally mentioned both the singer and the title he has given to his song.

Samuel Charters

1

In some of the larger cities of the American South there are still signs reading "White Only" painted on the doorways or windows of restaurants and laundries. Dingy clapboard barrooms have painted arrows, usually part of the advertising on the building front, reading "Colored Entrance," the arrow pointing to a back door or to a service window in the side of the building. At hospital entrances there are ornate metal letters reading "Out Patient Dispensary—Colored" and "Out Patient Dispensary—White." The doors are separate. In the smaller towns there usually aren't so many signs, except for the benches under the shade of an overhanging store marquee or at a bus stop. Someone who didn't know the town well, someone perhaps in from a nearby farm for some shopping, might get the benches confused. Sometimes drinking fountains are marked, and gasoline station rest rooms, but there usually isn't much need for signs since the townspeople, white and black, know every street and every store front and every foot of pavement, and their own place on it. If someone stops in the town he's expected to look around and find where the color line has been drawn. In northern cities the line is less definite, and the emotional response is less intense if the line is crossed, but within every neighborhood some blocks are black and others white. Even with an increased range of employment opening more and more to young black men and women, with neighborhood restrictions being slowly pushed aside, and with educational opportunities steadily increasing, the line, despite its seeming vagueness and lack of official sanction, is still tightly drawn. The life of the Negro and the life of his white neighbor is still separate and apart, and despite recent social progress will remain separate for many years to come.

The life of the Negro in America has been so completely lived on the other side of the racial line that it is only with difficulty that white and black can even understand each other's social attitudes. The Negro has been deprived of any large part in American life, despite the hundred years that have passed since the Civil War ended southern slavery. The inequality of opportunity, social and economic, is so extreme that a sensitive young Negro is forced into an almost intolerable emotional position, and it is only a slowly and painfully acquired set of defenses and self-justifications that makes it possible for him to even force himself to confront the indignity and the anger that is part of being a Negro in the United States.

From this separateness of white and Negro there has come not only differences in social attitude, but also in social expression. The lives of the two groups are so insistently kept apart that there has grown up within the Negro society its own artistic self-expression. There has been another strong influence on the self-expression of the Negro, his African cultural background, but this has been such a disadvantage to his social development that if there had been an opportunity to become part of the main stream of American life it probably would have been as quickly forgotten as the backgrounds and traditions of other groups whose standards and whose expressions have become mingled with the larger American attitudes. The Negro has been forced to remain apart. Already, from the separateness of expression which this has meant, have come the musical styles of jazz, which have strongly influenced the development of popular music everywhere in the world, and which may be the root force for a regeneration of the European classical tradition. Lesser known, but of perhaps as great significance, has been the development of a poetic expression of great strength and vividness, the blues.

With the blues the Negro subculture in the United States has its own popular music. As the two groups have adjusted uncomfortably to the separateness of their experience each of them has developed its own popular song, and the blues is to the black musician what conventional popular music is to the white. Its preoccupations are the concerns and the emotions of ordinary life. Since the audience for the blues, and for popular song, is often a young audience its most persistent theme is their overwhelming concern with the torment of love and their sudden consciousness of sexuality. There are other themes, the insecurity and difficulty of much of Negro life, the discomfort and loneliness of the enforced wandering of many of the singers, sometimes even a veiled protest at the social situation, but the most broadly woven strand in the texture of the blues is the despair of love. The blues is the song of men and women who have been hurt, who have been disappointed, who feel the confusion and the isolation of love. There

are blues which are insistent in their
promise of seduction, and there are
blues which are largely sexual boasts,
but the man who usually sings the
blues is the man who has found in love
only pain and disappointment. As the
Mississippi singer J. D. Short expressed
it,

*Well, the blues first came from people
being low in spirit and worried about
their loved ones.*

It is not in its subject, however, that
the blues has become poetic. Love is
just as much the theme of the popular
music of the larger society, but it is
difficult to think of American popular
song as having any of the freshness
and the vigor of poetry. It is in the
strength and vitality of its imagery and
expression that the blues has become
a poetic language. The language of
American popular song has lost its
freshness and its ability to convey
even strong emotion. The English folk
tradition which produced the broadside
ballads and the rich profusion of love
song and social commentary has dwin-
dled to a repetitive and almost meaningless manipulation of phrases which
no longer have even the artistic power
of the sentimental Victorian love poetry
from which they are derived. As the

years pass the blues may become as
moribund as popular song has become,
and as the developing blues audience
forces the singer into repetitions of his
own attitudes there is an increasing
tendency toward this, but the blues still
have a fine, raw vigor.

The blues does not try to express an
attitude toward the separateness of
Negro life in America. Protest is only a
small thread in the blues. But it is an
expression of the separateness of the
two racial groups. If the color line was
not drawn through the streets and the
neighborhoods of American cities the
blues would not have been developed.
There are religious people who strongly
oppose the blues, but the attitudes that
are expressed by the singers still mirror
the attitudes of the Negro community.
It is in some ways discomforting to
think of the blues as an expression of
"differentness," since it is the difference between Negro and white in America which has been used as the justifi-
cation for preventing the Negro from
taking his place in American society,
but there is a difference in tradition and
in the social memory which gives to
both blacks and whites their distinctive-
ness. The final measure of a democratic
society, however, is not its conformity,
but in its diversity, and there must be in

America a merging of the two communities, not necessarily into a group without differences, but into a single group that accepts these differences. It is then that the poetry of the blues will take its place as a force in the shaping of a new society, for in the blues will be found the expression of attitudes and beliefs that will become for the American Negro part of a racial memory, and part of a developing social history.

Since the blues is so much a reflection of the life in the segregated slums or the lonely farms where most of the Negro community still remains in the United States today is it possible for someone who is not a Negro to understand the language of the blues? In much of the blues there is a strong universality, and already American popular song has begun to take some of its material from it. There is no difficulty in understanding a verse like,

Did you ever wake up in the morning,
    find your man had gone?
Did you ever wake up in the morning,
    find your man had gone?
You will wring your hands, you will
    cry the whole day long.

But the blues which are most closely involved with the reality of being a Negro in the United States will always have emotional overtones which will be almost impossible to sense. No one who has not lived as a Negro in the Mississippi Delta can understand fully what the singer Son House meant to express when he sang,

My black woman's face shines like the sun.
My black woman's face shines like the sun.
Lipstick and powder sure can't help her none.

2

The blues sometimes seems to have traveled a long way before the earliest recordings helped to settle it down in the 1920's. There still seems to be some of the dust and the discomfort of the trip in a singer's voice, or in the imagery of a word or a line. The trip, however, hasn't been a long one. The formal patterns of the blues seem to have developed less than sixty years ago, sometime during the years before the First World War. It is the blues' intensity and directness, its response to the reality of experience, which gives it a traveled appearance. It has been so many generations since European and American popular song has had the immediacy of the blues that there is a tendency to think of the earliest blues as somehow part of this almost forgotten period of history. But in the verses, and in the musical styles, there is still a young, fresh vitality. Many of the older men who remember the blues are still living. Some of them even still sing. They live on back streets in southern cities like Memphis or St. Louis, on run-down farms, in smaller towns like Spartanburg or Macon. Some of them have drifted into the slums of New York or Chicago. Some of them have day jobs, a few have become businessmen, somehow finding a footing in the shifting patterns of southern racial discrimination; others live on welfare checks. Most of them are poorly educated, often broken physically by the long years of menial work or by the drain of long and enthusiastic dissipation. With strangers they often have difficulty in expressing themselves in conversation, but there is one subject on which all of them have definite and carefully considered feelings: the blues.

They don't travel as much as they did when they were younger; when a "travelin' mood" would set them drifting from town to town until they settled with a new job or a new woman. They don't see each other as much and they don't have as much chance to sing together, but their attitudes toward the blues have a marked similarity. Their concern is with the sincerity of the blues. They think of the blues as an expression of the difficulties and the disappointments of the life that they have seen in the streets and tenements and the poor farms. Henry Townsend, in St. Louis, felt that the heart of the blues was ". . . the true feeling." Furry Lewis, in Memphis said ". . . all the blues, you can say, is true." As J. D. Short expressed it,

What I think about that makes the blues really good is when a fellow writes a blues and then writes it with a feeling, with great harmony, and there's so many true words in the blues, of things that have happened to so many people, and that's why it makes the feeling in the blues.

The blues, as a poetic language, has still the direct, immediate relationship to experience that is at the heart of all art. It is here that poetry begins, in the response of the artist to life. As the art develops it becomes self-conscious and self-concerned, and the poetic language begins to imitate itself. Instead of a direct concern with experience there is a concern with the conventions and the restrictions of the forms which the earlier artists have found. This will happen to the language of the blues, as it happens to any art, but for men like Furry Lewis and J. D. Short, the blues were a new response to the reality of their lives. As the Negro community slowly developed a shape and a self-consciousness in the late years of the 19th century it was the blues that developed with it to express the confusion and the joy and the pain of living in this community, related to the white society economically, but separated from it, and from the conventions that concerned its popular song, by the line of prejudice.

Many of the singers, in their concern with sincerity, feel that not only must the blues have a "true feeling," but that it is the singer himself who must have the emotional experience that the blues expresses. Memphis Willie B. said, "A blues is about something that's real. It's about what a man feels when his wife leaves him, or about some disappointment that happens to him that he can't do anything about. That's why none of these young boys can really sing the blues. They don't know about the things that go into a blues." When asked what was the quality that made a good blues singer, Henry Townsend simply laughed.

Trouble . . . that's right. That's the one-word solution. Trouble. You know you can only express a true feeling if you're sincere about it. You can only express what happened to you.

Baby Tate, in Spartanburg, South Carolina, felt that it was ". . . difficul-

ties. I don't put it all on drinking or
nothing like that, I put it on difficulty in
your home." Furry Lewis didn't even
think of the writing of the blues as
separate from the emotions of the blues.

*Well, one thing, when you write the
blues and what you be thinking about,
you be blue and you ain't got nothing
hardly to think about. You just already
blue, and you just go on and write.*

From this directness of expression
have come the dominant themes of the
blues: love, disappointment, and anger.
In the blues the singer finds a release
from his emotions. As Baby Tate put it,

*I'll tell you what gives me the blues.
When my wife makes me mad. Make
me angry otherwise. A dog go mad.
But if she makes me angry. I didn't do
all I can do or something like that, and
she want me to do something else. She
get me angry. Well, the first thing I do
I'll grab my guitar and walk out of the
house to keep from having a fight . . .*

J. D. Short nodded when he was
asked if singing helped him to get
through periods of emotional stress.

*Yes, it actual do. It's a lot of times we
can get very worried and dissatisfied,*

and we can get to singing the blues and
if we can play music and play the blues
we may play the blues for a while until
we get kind of pacified. That cuts off a
lot of worry.

And, as he went on to say, there is
also an emotional release for the person
listening to the blues.

Sometimes the people that's listening
at you have actual been through some
of the same things that I have been
through and automatically that takes
effect on them and that causes their
attention to come.

Henry Townsend described his own
feelings about the blues, saying,

When you express yourself, how you
felt, how you been mistreated, and the
things that happened to you in life,
that's the only thing you can say. If you
sing anything else then you're singing
something somebody else has felt.

Then he went on to explain how, as a
musician, he can reach the emotions of
an audience with something that someone else has written.

Now some writer might walk up and
tell you, "Here's a song I want you to

sing. *Play it cheap, if you want, but it's
the truth."* He wants you to sing it because he's not able to and he'd like it to
be done, and if you're sincere enough
about taking sympathy with the fellow
you can do the song for him.

For these men the language of the
blues has the directness and the sincerity of their own experience. Even the
dominant theme of the blues, the torment and the pain of love, reflects this
immediacy of response to life. To Furry
Lewis,

*. . . the blues come from a woman
wanting to see her man, and a man
wanting to see his woman.*

And, as Henry Townsend said with a
shrug,

*You know, that's the major thing in
life. Please believe me. What you love
the best is what can hurt you the
most . . .*

The poetic language of the blues
reflects this immediacy of experience.
It is a terse idiom, as direct and un-
adorned as the whine of a guitar string.
A blues often has as few as a dozen
lines, but within this restricted area the
emotional statement is still rich and
vivid. Much of the power of the blues

expression is in the relationship between the stanzas, but the stanzas, or verses, as most singers would call them, have a completeness of thought within themselves. The verse, rather than the line or the couplet, is the poetic brick out of which the structure of the blues is built. The earliest blues verses developed from the shouted work songs of the field and the prison yard. The lead singer would call,

Well, you know I left my woman,

the men would respond with a rhythmic phrase that emphasized their work movements, "Here, Rattler, Here," "Hammer Ring," "Good God A'Mighty"; then the singer would either repeat the line or finish the phrase with a line like,

She's standin' at the station.

The entire phrase would be,

Well, you know I left my woman,
    Hammer Ring!
She's standin' at the station
    Hammer Ring!

It was a casual, freely improvised form, but there was occasionally some concern with rhyme, and there would be phrases like,

*You ought to heard what that letter
        read,
    Here, Rattler, here!
That letter says my woman's dead,
    Here, Rattler, here!*

If the caller were to sing it by himself,
it would be a rude blues verse,

*You ought to heard what that letter
        read,
That letter says my woman's dead.*

Among the early blues recordings
were several which still used the two
line verse.

*Lay awake and just can't eat a bite.
She used to be my rider, but she just
        won't treat me right.*

A work song verse, from the Angola
Penitentiary in Louisiana,

*Mister governor don't you hear me,
    My hammer ring!
You know I wants to go home.
    My hammer ring!*

becomes as a blues verse,

*I wrote the Governor to please turn me
        loose,*

> Since I didn't get no answer I know it
> ain't no use.

Sometimes the verses were even used
unrhymed, as in Bullet Williams'
"Touch Me Light Mama,"

> I believe to my soul, got to leave your
> town.
> I ain't got no pretty mama, so talk to
> me.

but for most singers the use of rhyme is
an essential part of the blues language.
As Furry Lewis put it,

> The time when you get a blues, what
> you call the blues, you just haven't
> come out like you s'posed to and it
> don't be right. You have to go all over
> it again until you rhyme it. It got to be
> rhymed up if you call yourself being
> with the blues. If it ain't rhymed up it
> don't sound good to me or nobody else.

There is, however, a free use of near
rhyme. Most singers are more concerned with the strength of the verse
than they are with the exactness of the
rhyme. Some of the more common near
rhymes are close in sound, "man" and
"hand," "ground" and "down," "dime"
and "mine." Others have a looser rela-

tionship. "Ride" and "by," "town" and
"now," "deep" and "week." Sometimes
the soft pronunciation forces a rhyme
between two words that are different in sound. "Before" is usually pro-
nounced "befo," and with this sound it
is used to rhyme with "go" and "slow."
Most singers would agree with Furry,
"If it ain't rhymed up it don't sound
good to me or nobody else," but there
is considerable flexibility in the use of
rhyming words and phrases.

It was with the development of the
three line verse that the blues became
a distinctive poetic form, and it is the
singer who first used it, whose name
will never be known, who should be
thought of as the father of the blues. It
may have first been used by some
singer who was improvising his songs,
someone at a country dance, playing in
the flickering light of a kerosene lantern
as the couples stamped past him. As it
got later, and as he got tired, he ran out
of songs and began singing odd
phrases from the hollers and gang
chants. He had to put together lines
that rhymed, and by repeating the first
line he had a moment to think about
his last line, the rhyming line. At first it
may have been used with halting emphasis, the repetition little more than a
half-sung imitation of the first line, but

in the repeated first line is the strength
of the blues verse, and as singers began to use it with a more intense expression, emphasizing the emotion of
the first line, the blues took on a new
depth and color. The thought is still
complete within the first and third lines,

*Times is so tough, can't even get a
dime,*
*Times don't get better, I'm going to lose
my mind.*

but with the repetition of the first line
the verse, little more than a simple couplet, becomes the more expressive full
stanza.

*Times is so tough, can't even get a
dime.*

There is an insistence in the singer's
voice as he sings again,

*Yes, times is so tough, can't even get a
dime.*

Then he decides,

*Times don't get better, I'm going to lose
my mind.*

As the line is repeated it takes on a
new emphasis, and with the delayed

completion of the phrase there is a
suspense, even if only momentary, before the resolution of the final line. The
verse becomes even more of a dramatic
entity as the singer uses the musical
phrase to further emphasize the repetition, changing the harmony under the
second line to a subdominant chord
which moves to a resolution as the line
ends. The poetic device is a simple one,
but it is remarkably effective as a result
of its simplicity. It is a unique verse
form, and within it have developed the
richest strains of blues poetry.

Although the three line verse is char-
acteristic of the blues there is still a use
of other verse forms, and they give to
the blues a necessary variety. Sometimes the two line phrase is broken mu-
sically into four shorter phrases, and
the verse changes from,

*I was standing on the corner with my
        hat in my hand,
Looking for a woman didn't have no
        man,*

to,

*I was standing on the corner,
I had my hat in my hand.
I was looking for a woman,
Woman without a man.*

It is a less dramatic stanza, but it is very effective for the faster blues, when the singer is shouting over a noisy accompaniment. It is often used in a form of blues recitative, when the singer uses two melodic and rhythmic patterns within the same verse. He begins with a half-spoken recitative that takes the place of the first line, half speaking, half singing it with a rhythmic phrase that is half the length of the other two lines that finish the verse,

You know my woman left me,
Left me cold in hand.
I wouldn't hate it so bad,
but she left with another man.

then he returns to the slower tempo for the next two lines,

I want to know, I want to know why did
*   my baby go.*
I love that woman, love her 'til it hurts
*   me so.*

Often the last two lines are repeated for every verse, almost as a refrain, while the first four half-spoken lines become the developing idea. Lightning Hopkins often uses this form, and he has developed it into a vivid personal language. Usually he begins with a conventional verse that sketches out his idea,

*I say go bring me my shotgun, bring me
          back some shells
I say go bring me my shotgun, bring me
          back a pocket full of shells.
Yes, if I don't get some competition you
          know there's gonna be trouble
          here.*

In his second verse he uses the four line
recitative stanza, ending with the last
two lines of the first verse.

*Yes, you know my woman tried to
          quit me,
When I ain't done nothing wrong,
She done put me out of doors, boy,
And I ain't even got no home.
I said just bring me my shotgun, boy,
          you can bring me just one or two
          shells.
Yes, if I don't get some competition you
          know there's gonna be trouble
          here.*

As his idea is developed the use of the
last two lines as a refrain gives to his
blues a strong sense of unity, and with
the four line stanza he has a wider
range of poetic expression available to
him.

Occasionally there have been singers who have used an unusual verse
pattern, and in some of these individual
forms there has often been an imaginative development of the blues language.

One of the most moving blues of the
Memphis singer Will Shade uses a
complex stanza that has two four line
groups within the verse.

What you going to do, Mama,
When your troubles get like mine?
Take a mouthful of sugar,
And drink a bottle of turpentine.
I can't stand it.
I can't stand it.
Drop down, Mama,
Sweet as the showers of rain.

The Mississippi singer Bukka White
used a six line verse for a rushing,
shouted blues,

Look over yonder,
On the burying ground,
On the burying ground,
Look over yonder,
On the burying ground.
Yon' stand ten thousand standin' to see
them let me down.

Even the three line stanza has been
used as the basis for an individual poetic statement. Another Mississippi
singer, the great Robert Johnson, extended the stanza by repeating the last
phrase of each line for one of his most
intense blues.

I got to keep moving, I got to keep
       moving,
          blues falling down like hail, blues
          falling down like hail.
Uunh, blues falling down like hail,
       blues falling down like hail,
And the day keeps on 'minding me
       there's a
          hellhound on my trail,
          hellhound on my trail,
          hellhound on my trail.

I can tell the wind is rising, the leaves
       trembling on the trees,
       trembling on the trees.
I can tell the wind is rising, the leaves
       trembling on the trees,
       uunh.
All I need my little sweet woman, to
       keep
          my company,
          uunh,
          my company.

Furry Lewis, in describing how he wrote a blues, felt that almost any verse could be used to begin a song.

The first verse could be the last. You know, just any old verse that I wanted I could make that the first, then go right on from there and just rhyme up from it and make them all kind of match, you know.

By making them "match" he meant relating them by idea.

Just like if I was to rhyme something, if I was to have a song now, and say, "Bye, bye, I got no more to say." Well that could be the first verse, and then the next verse I could say, "I'm sorry, baby, you treat me this'a way." That'd be in a different verse altogether, and the next would go on, you know, just like that. You want all the verses to be talking about the same thing.

Most blues are constructed from verses that have a relationship in mood or attitude. The directness of the blues is a directness of emotional expression. An incident, "Bye, Bye, I got no more to say," begins a train of attitudes suggested by the incident's implications, "I'm sorry, baby, you treat me this'a way." There is little concern in the blues for the narrated event. There have been occasional blues which told a story, but the popular narrative songs have been the well-known ballads, "John Henry," "Stagolee," "Frankie and Albert," "Betty and Dupree," and "Bo'-Weevil." Several of the country singers recorded narrative blues in the '20's, but the limitations of the recording usually restricted them to a few verses and the performances were incomplete. Charlie

Patton, from the Mississippi delta, recorded a group of verses about his arrest and imprisonment in Belzoni, Mississippi.

When the trial's in Belzoni ain't no use
a feeling proud,
When the trial is in Belzoni, ain't no use
a feeling proud,
Mr. Ware will take you by the Belzoni
jailhouse for life.

Let me tell you, folks, how he treated
me,
Let me tell you, folks, how he treated
me,
An' he put me in the cellar where the
donkey used to be.

It was late one evening, Mr. Purvis was
standing around.
It was late one evening, Mr. Purvis was
standing around.
Mr. Purvis told Mr. Ware, sir, please
let poor Charlie down.

It takes a boozey booze, Lord, to carry
me through,
It takes a boozey booze, Lord, to car' me
through.
Purvis took me to yon' jailhouse, where
there is no booze.

Difficulties with local sheriffs and

judges were such an ordinary experience for many southern Negroes that there were several narrative blues similar to Patton's. Willie Newburn, from Shelby County, Tennessee, sang,

> Well, I left Margrit, on the way back to
>   Memphis, Tennessee.
> Well, I left Margrit, on the way back to
>   Memphis, Tennessee.
> No sooner I got at the bus station, Lord,
>   the police he arrest poor me.

> Lord, the police arrest me, carried me
>   before the judge.
> Police 'rest me, take me 'fore the judge.
> Well, the law talks so fast I didn't have
>   time to say nary a word.

> Well, the lawyer plead and the judge
>   he wrote it down,
> Lawyer pleaded and the judge he wrote
>   it down.
> Says I'll give you ten days, buddy,
>   down in little Shelby town . . .

Probably Sleepy John Estes used the narrative blues with the most success. He has always been interested in the small details of his experience, and they often give his verses a remarkable presence. Sometimes the scene is recalled so vividly that there seems to be the sound of a train rattling over a switch or the smell of the wind from the fields in a line or phrase. He was able to express the immediacy of the experience within a few verses by selecting the details for their emotional effect. He has described the near drowning that was the subject for his "Floating Bridge."

I was travelin' in Hickman, Kentucky and the car went in the high water, the '37 flood it was. Got going to my cousin's home and had to go across one of them floating bridges tied to the cable there, you know, to keep it from floating away, and we got on that bridge and hit that pretty rough, you know, the way he was driving. He lost control of the car and it went off to the left. I was sitting on the far side putting some strings in my shoes and I was the last one. There's two-three on the other side of me and that made me last getting out on the bridge.

Well, my cousin, it knocked him in the head scuffling in the car. He cut hisself and he's sitting up there on a log and he asks, "Everybody out?" "Unun, John's still in there." By that time I had come up the third time. He jumped off that board and saved me. He got me and put me under his arm and treaded water up to the bridge and pulled me up on to it.

From this experience he has taken the
details which have the most immediate
emotional effect and developed them
into a brilliant blues.

Now I never will forget that floating
  bridge.
Now I never will forget that floating
  bridge.
Now I never will forget that floating
  bridge.
Tell me five minutes' time in the water
  I was hid.

When I was going down I throwed up
  my hands.
When I was going down I throwed up
  my hands.
When I was going down I throwed up
  my hands.
Please take me on dry land.

Now they carried me in the house and
  they laid me 'cross the bank.
Now they carried me in the house and
  they laid me 'cross the bank.
Now they carried me in the house and
  they laid me 'cross the bank.
'Bout a gallon and a half of muddy
  water I had drank.

They dried me off and they laid me in
  the bed.

*Now they dried me off and they laid me
in the bed.*
*Now they dried me off and they laid me
in the bed.*
*Couldn't hear nothing but muddy water
running through my head.*

*Now my mother often taught me, quit
playing a bum.*
*Now my mother often taught me, quit
playing a bum.*
*Now my mother often taught me, quit
playing a bum.*
*Go somewhere, settle down and make
a crop.*

*Now the people standing on the bridge
was screaming and crying.*
*Now the people on the bridge was
screaming and crying.*
*Now the people on the bridge standing
screaming and crying.*
Lord, have mercy while we gwine.

The blues which are developed out
of verses related by their emotional
mood are the simplest for a singer to
put together, and much of the poetry of
the blues uses this form. The difficulty
in using verses that have only an emotional relationship is in creating a verse
pattern that is personal and intense.
Because so much of the blues is concerned with the disappointments of

love there are hundreds of verses using
this idea, and a singer can simply put
four or five of these second-hand verses
together and have a blues that will
have little individuality but will give
him something to sing without much
effort involved. Most of the singers who
record a great deal exhaust their store
of original ideas very quickly and
spend the rest of their careers repeating the conventional verses until they
become as meaningless and banal as
the popular music of the larger American culture. As in the other popular arts
it is personality that distinguishes the
successful artist, not musicianship or
imagination. In the hands of a minor
blues singer this arrangement of verses
by association can become dull and
trite, but a sensitive singer can use the
form with considerable success. Bessie
Tucker began one of her finest blues
with a verse describing the incident that
started her train of thought.

Hey, hey, hey, what's the matter with
     my man today?
Hey, hey, hey, what's the matter with
     my man today?
I asked him if he loved me, and he
     walked away.

In her second verse she has moved on
to her anger at the insult, and con-

siders what might happen to her if she
gave way to her feelings.

*Penitentiar', Penitentiar', hey, is going
to be my home.   (Penitentiary)
Penitentiar', Penitentiar', hey, is going
to be my home.
Because my man he mistreated me,
Lord he have done me wrong.*

With a shake of her head she wryly
considers her situation.

*The man that I'm 'a loving, Lord, is
going to get me killed.
The man that I'm 'a loving, Lord, is
going to get me killed.
Because love is a proposition that's got
many a poor girl killed.*

She has made a general statement, but
it is related to the other verses by her
own involvement in the situation. It is
an emotional association, and it is effective in extending her attitude. She finishes the blues with an open threat to
her lover, for his "pallin' " with other
women,

*I love you, hey, but you won't behave.
I love you, hey, but you won't behave.
You going to keep on a pallin', going to
wake up in your grave.*

her voice expressing her disappointment and anger.

In many of the blues which use ar-
rangements of verses to develop emotional attitudes there is often a power of
suggestion in the juxtaposition of verses
that seem to have little relationship.
This poetic technique has been used by
several modern poets as a conscious
artistic device, and it gives to the blues
singers the same technical control over
their material. They use it most often to
compress their idiom, to imply, with the
juxtaposition of verses, an association
of events that would take several verses
to explain and would lose the dramatic
effect in the explanation. Often the
blues seems to be only the lightly
sketched outline of an emotional tur-
moil that, like the finest drawing, would
be overwhelming if it were to be developed into a full composition. The
sketch is sometimes so vague that it is
difficult to decide on the meaning of a
particular line, and the singers themselves, because the poetic language of
the blues has been part of their lives,
often feel that the only meaning of the
line is its own sense. But the imaginative power of the blues is still felt even
when the meaning is obscure. In his
blues, "My Black Woman," Son House,
another singer from the Mississippi
Delta, began with two verses that had
an obvious relationship in their concern
with a letter, but they are two separate

verses which have been juxtaposed to
heighten the mood of the song.

*Well, did you get that letter I mailed in
        your back yard?*
Uumh, that I mailed in your back yard?
*It's mighty sad to say that your best
        friend we have got to part.*

*Well, I got a letter this morning, how do
        you reckon it read?*
*Got a letter this morning, how do you
        reckon it read?*
*"Better hurry, hurry, 'cause the gal you
        love is dead."*

In the first verse someone is singing
that they have left a letter in a back
yard, and in the second verse someone
else, both referring to themselves as "I,"
has gotten a letter. Since the blues goes
on to make it clear that the person singing the second verse is Son House the
person singing the first verse has to be
someone else. It could be the person
who left the letter which Son opens and
reads, and it is indefinite; since "we
have got to part" is often used to describe death as well as separation, but
there is almost a suggestion of tenderness in the first verse, and the last line
could be phrased, "It's mighty sad to
say that we have got to part." In the
second verse it is clear that the woman
he loves is not near him; since it has

taken a letter to tell him of her death,
so the first verse seems to be the voice
of the woman as she asks him about
the letter she left telling him that she
had to leave. He has drawn an outline
of their love and separation in strokes so
faint as to be almost unnoticeable, but
the interrelationship of the two verses
has developed an entire emotional situation in a brief moment of song. The
verses that ended the blues have the
immediacy of experience and the directness of expression that marks the
greatest blues, using the simple three
line verse that is the blues' unique con-
tribution to the forms of modern poetry.

You know I got my suitcase and I took
    on down the road,
Uumh, took on down the road,
But when I got there she was laying on
    the cooling bo'd.

You know I walked up close and I
    looked down in her face,
Uumh I looked down in her face.
You a good old gal, but you got to lay
    down to judgement day.

You know, I fold my arms and I slowly
    walk away.
Uumh, I slowly walk away.
You a good old gal, I just can't take
    your place.

3

Within the blues there is a conscious use of the poetic devices that have been for centuries part of the English poetic tradition. Although the idea of a blues verse may be relatively simple the language which expresses it has often a marked sophistication. The directness and immediacy of the experience is heightened with an imagery and a symbolism that is itself drawn from the reality of the life. It is a poetic idiom that finds its images in the cabins and the tenements, in the fields, the empty roads, and the crowded streets of American Negro life.

The simile, the direct comparison, is used often in blues verses. One of the earliest lines, used in blues in every part of the South, was the well-known,

*My woman has a heart like a stone
            cast in the sea . . .*

A line still used in Mississippi and Tennessee is the vivid,

*Put your arms around me like the
circle 'round the sun . . .*

The singer who first compared the
"circle 'round the sun" with the warmth
and the intensity of an embrace found
his comparison in the sun over his head
as he stood in the summer fields, just as
Blind Lemon Jefferson, in describing a
woman, found his comparison in the
movements of the squirrels in the
brush along the stream beds in Texas
where he had been raised,

*She's a fair made woman, cunning as
a squirrel . . .*

The metaphor, the indirect comparison, is less often used, but it still is
found in many blues. Big Joe Williams
sings,

*Before I be your dog, before I be your
dog,
'Fore I be your dog, if I had my way,
Make you walk the log . . .*

Like much of blues metaphor this
could be read as an image, rather than
an indirect comparison, but the distinc-
tion between the two is often slight and
depends on the singer's interpretation.
If Big Joe meant "Before I be (like) your
dog," then the phrase is a metaphor,

but if he meant, "Before I (let you treat
me the way you treat) your dog," then
he intended it as an image. There is
such an extended use of imagery in the
blues that it has taken the place of
metaphor as a dominant poetic device.

Personification, giving to an object or
an idea the characteristics of a human
being, has always been important in
the blues, and even in some early work
song verses the "blues" itself has already become almost human. By the
late 1920's Lonnie Johnson could sing,

*People, I've stood these blues 'bout as
  long as I can.*
*I walked all night with these blues, we
  both joined hand in hand.*
*And they travelled my heart through,
  just like a natural man.*

referring to the blues as someone he
could walk all night with ". . . joined
hand in hand." In other verses, however, the word is still used in the Eliza-
bethan sense of "blue devils." It is this
meaning that is intended in the widely
known verse,

*Woke up this morning, blues all 'round
  my bed,*
*Woke up this morning, blues all 'round
  my bed,*

Picked up my pillow, blues all under
my head.

In Blind Willie McTell's verse,

Blues grabbed me at midnight, didn't
turn me loose 'til day,
Blues grabbed me at midnight, didn't
turn me loose 'til day,
I didn't have no mama to drive these
blues away,

it could be the blues personified as a
human figure that seized him, or the
"blue devils," or simply the mood of the
blues. One of the most vivid of the per-
sonifications of the blues is Ma Rainey's
"Yonder Comes The Blues," in which
she seems to suggest that the blues is a
loiterer, lounging after her when she
tries to ignore his presence.

I worry all day, I worry all night,
Everytime my man comes home he
wants to fuss and fight,
When I pick up the paper to try to read
the news,
Just when I'm satisfied, yonder comes
the blues.

I went down to the river each and every
day,
Trying to keep from throwing myself
away.

*I walked and I walked 'til I wore out my
      shoes,
I can't walk no further, yonder comes
      the blues . . .*

*People have the different blues and
      think they're mighty sad,
But blues about a man the worst I ever
      had.
I been disgusted and all confused,
Every time I look around, yonder comes
      the blues.*

There is as much use made of the
closely related technique of apostrophe,
in which something inanimate is ad-
dressed as human. A prison gang,
working in a ragged line in the after-
noon heat, sings to "Old Hannah," the
sun.

*Oh, go down, old Hannah,
      Well, well, well
Don't you rise no more.
      Don't you rise no more.
Why don't you go down, old Hannah,
      Old Hannah,
Don't you rise,
      No more.*

Hociel Thomas, accompanying herself
on the piano, sings,

> Go down, sunshine, and see what
>   tomorrow brings.
> Go down, sunshine, and see what
>   tomorrow brings.
> Lord, he might bring sunshine, then
>   again he might bring rain.

With the extended train imagery of many blues there is often a verse in which the singer addresses the train, trying to make it listen to him as it pulls away from the station with his woman.

> I'm crying, "Train, train, bring my baby
>   back to me."
> Hear me crying, "Train, train, bring my
>   baby back to me.
> Can't bring back my baby just bring me
>   my used-to-be."

Even the less-well-known technique of metonymy, the use of a related idea for the idea itself, is often found in the blues. The expression "I'm going to put on my traveling shoes," has become almost a cliché, but the use of the word "traveling" to imply that the singer is thinking of leaving is an obvious use of metonymy. The phrase has been used so often that "traveling" has little more effect than an adjective, but a similar phrase in a less familiar blues still has the vividness of the stronger figure of speech. As Sleepy John Estes sings,

*I'm going upstairs and pack my
        leaving trunk . . .*

The imagery of the blues has a rich
variety of expression, and in it is the
directness of an immediately imagined
poetic idea. Cat-Iron, an intense Mississippi singer recorded by Frederic Ram-
sey Jr. in Natchez, knew what it meant
to be left by someone, and he knew the
sound of muffled crying in the night.
Instead of singing,

*I got something to tell you going to
        make you cry . . .*

he sang,

*I got something to tell you, woman,
        make the hair rise on your head.*

*I got something to tell you, woman,
        make the hair rise on your head.
I got something to tell you, woman,
        make the spring cry on your
        bed . . .*

Furry Lewis, instead of promising his
woman that he would make her rich,
promises her that he will make her
money grow like the grass on a spring
field.

*If you'll be my woman I will turn your
        money green.*

If you'll be my woman I will turn your
money green.
Show you more money, baby, than
Rockefeller ever seen.

Tommy McClennan, standing beside
a road in the Mississippi delta, waiting
for a bus, sees it coming toward him
and for a moment the swaying Greyhound becomes, in his imagination, a
dog running along the road in the hot
sun.

Here comes that Greyhound with his
tongue hanging out on the side.
Here comes that Greyhound with his
tongue hanging out on the side.
You have to buy a ticket if you want to
ride.

In the pain of separation Gertrude
Perkins feels the desolation of a winter
wind.

The cold wind howling, howling in my
heart.
The wind howling, howling in my heart.
For the best of friends, Lord, they have
got to part.

Will Shade, sitting in his shabby
room behind Beale Street in Memphis,
tries to show the pain that his woman
has caused him.

If I could just take
My heart in my hand,
I could show you, woman,
How you treat a man . . .

The Black Ace, recording for Chris
Strachwitz with his old-fashioned steel
guitar in his home in Fort Worth, uses
the language of the card game to tell
his woman that she won't find a better
man.

I'm the Black Ace, I'm the boss card in
        your hand.
I'm the Black Ace, I'm the boss card in
        your hand.
But I'll play for you, mama, if you
        please let me be your man.

The imagery of the blues still has a
vitality and strength of expression.

In some of the greatest blues the
imagery has been extended into a symbolism in which the image becomes
something beyond itself, in which it has
a meaning beyond the immediate reality. Much of the sexual poetry of the
blues uses a colorful imagery and an
irrepressible symbolism, and it is such
a rich area of the blues that it will need
a fuller discussion to do it justice. In
many well-known blues, however, there

is an intense symbolism. In a folk culture, where little is written and there isn't a concern with precise meanings, the symbolism often becomes confused, but it continues to have some meaning for the singer who uses it, even though he would have a difficult time explaining it. Sometimes the symbol becomes so loose in its interpretation that the meaning changes within a few verses. The ballad song, "Careless Love," is sung by many blues performers, and as they alter it to the blues idiom there is considerable confusion about the term "careless love" itself. Although it seems to be a synonym for a heedless infatuation it has become "Kelly's love" in some versions, in others it seems to mean the sexual embrace, and in an imaginative version by Lonnie Johnson it becomes the symbol of everything that has menaced his life. Careless love has "robbed me out of my silver and gold," "caused my father to lose his mind," "drove me out in the ice and snow," and in the final verse Lonnie finally turns on this personification of his misfortunes with the words,

... Damn you, I'm going to shoot you.
Shoot you four or five times.
Then stand over you until you finish
        dying.

Even in the blues which have a con-
sistent symbolism there is often an
elaboration of the original idea which
confuses the meaning, but in a language which is still developing there is
often more variety than consistency. In
one of her finest blues Bessie Smith uses
the "long old road" as a symbol for the
passing years, and in her first verse
seems to have almost a religious intent
as she sings of meeting a friend. It is
similar to many spiritual verses.

*It's a long old road, but I'm gonna find
   the end.*
*It's a long old road, but I'm gonna find
   the end.*
*And when I get there I'm gonna shake
   hands with a friend.*

She continues to develop the symbol of
the road in a blues of great clarity and
power.

*On the side of the road I sat underneath
   the tree.*
*On the side of the road I sat underneath
   the tree.*
*Nobody knows the thoughts that come
   over me.*

*Weepin' and cryin', tears falling on the
   ground.*

Weepin' and cryin', tears falling on the
 ground.
When I got to the end I was so worried
 down.

Picked up my bag, baby, and I tried it
 again.
Picked up my bag, baby, and I tried it
 again.
I got to make it, I've got to find the end.

In the third verse there is a momentary confusion. She sings, "When I got
to the end I was so worried down." She
seems to imply that she's reached the
end of the road, but in the fourth verse
she ". . . tried it again . . . I've got to
find the end," so the line seems to mean
that she reached the end of her momentary depression, that she has cried
away her despair and is ready to begin
walking again. It is a moving use of a
symbol to express an involved idea of
the passage of life and the difficulty of
going on with it, and the thought is complete within its handful of lines. It is
often sung with this meaning, and with
this symbolism implied in the perform-
ance. Bessie, however, sings one more
verse, and almost succeeds in stripping
it of any poetic intent. Her last verse
finishes,

*You can't trust nobody, you might as
 well be alone.*
*You can't trust nobody, you might as
 well be alone.*
*Found my lost friend, and I might as
 well stayed at home.*

The literalness of the last verse im-
plies that she never intended to describe anything more than walking
along a road with a suitcase to see a
friend, and that there is no symbolic
meaning to the difficult journey she has
started. The blues, however, still has
the strength of inconsistency, and other
singers have used her symbol of the
"long old road" for their own lives,
overlooking the intent of her last verse.
The most imaginative of the singers
have a technical control of their idiom
which enables them to use not only the
words and phrases of simile and metaphor, of personification, apostrophe and
metonymy, but also the longer forms of
the image and the symbol. For Robert
Johnson the road, in his phrase the
"passway," became an intense and
moving symbolic expression of the
struggles that haunted his short life:

*I got stones in my passway, and my
 road seems dark as night.*
*I got stones in my passway, and my
 road seems dark as night.*

I have pains in my heart, they have
    taken my appetite.

I have a bird to whistle, and I have a
    bird to sing.
Have a bird to whistle, and I have a
    bird to sing.
I got a woman that I'm loving, boy, but
    she don't mean a thing.

My enemies have betrayed me, have
    overtaken poor Bob at last.
My enemies have betrayed me, have
    overtaken poor Bob at last.
And there's one thing certain, they have
    stones all in my path.

Now you are trying to take my life
And all my loving too.
You laid the passway for me,
Now what are you trying to do?
I'm crying, "Please, please, let us be
    friends,
And when you hear the howling in my
    passway, honey, please don't let
    me in."

4

Although the blues has always been
an expression of the attitudes and experiences of the Negro community in
America it has never been accepted by
the entire social group. Among both religious people and among the growing
middle class professional groups there
is often a dislike or a disinterest in the
blues. The religious feeling is very
strong, and in the South many singers
who have become church members are
reluctant to perform anything except
church music. The preoccupations of
the blues; love, sexuality, personal disappointment and unhappiness are felt
to be an insistent reminder of the world-
ly life that the Christian should forget.
This is a much stronger interpretation of
Christian doctrine than the larger white
society regards as necessary, but from
his side of the color line it has always
been obvious to the Negro that the
"Christianity" of American society has
never been more than a self-satisfied
delusion. An objection that the religious
people have made to the blues is that
it isn't "true." Since they are thinking in

57

terms of spiritual truth they have some
reason for their attitude, but the singers
object to this, feeling that the truth of
experience is as valid as the revealed
truth of religion. As Henry Townsend
put it,

You know, I'm going to put this a
little blunt. I don't know if I should say
it or not, because it might hurt the religious type of people, but when I sing
the blues I sing the truth. The religious
type of people may not believe that it's
good, because they think the blues is
not the truth; but the blues, from a point
of explaining yourself as facts, is the
truth, and I don't feel that the truth
should be condemned . . .

The concerns of the blues, however,
are not the concerns of the religious
community, and the music is not an
expression of their life and experience.

The attitudes of the professional
groups, the growing intellectual class
within the Negro society, are also not
expressed in the blues. Except for the
restrictions which face any Negro in
America, regardless of his education
or social background, their life is little
different from that of other middle-class
Americans. Sometimes there is a strong
dislike for the blues, since in its rough-

ness and directness there is persistent
reminder of the years of squalid slavery
and semislavery, but there is more
often just disinterest. Either they listen
to conventional popular music or they
listen to classical music. The life of the
blues is a hard, amoral, lonely life, and
its reality is a harsh, unrelenting strug-
gle with poverty, jealousy and disappointment. It is not the life of a settled
middle-class community. The earliest
blues singers were what J. D. Short
called "good time men." They were the
drifters, the malcontents, the shiftless
stragglers. They lived on society's lowest level, in the world of prostitution,
illegitimacy, dishonesty, casual sexuality, and police brutality. By the time
Short had become a young man and
was singing in Clarksdale, Mississippi,
the blues singer could be a hard-working and fairly successful entertainer,
and younger singers today often live in
a professional environment that would
be strange and uncomfortable for someone like Charlie Patton, who moved
from cabin to cabin in the Mississippi delta, singing whenever anyone
handed him a guitar and turning up at
crossroads and country stores on Satur-
day nights to earn a little money singing.
The audience for the blues, however, is
still the people at this lowest level; although the blues language is under-

stood by nearly every Negro in the United States and occasional recordings will sell to a more general audience. For the people who listen to the blues, life still has the directness and the vividness which the blues express. In the poetry of the blues they find the frightening despair or the sudden ecstasy of their experience.

The singers have always felt this relationship with their audiences, and it is this feeling that is behind their insistence on the blues as "truth." Many of the greatest singers still keep their roots in the ragged life of the Negro slums. As Memphis Willie B. implied, when he said the young men can't sing the blues because they don't know about the emotions that go into the blues, it is necessary to be involved with this life to reach the most intensely creative level of the blues. Lightning Hopkins, despite his years as a successful performer for audiences in universities and consciously artistic night clubs, returns to Houston between jobs and works on weekends in the local "juke joints." In the summer of 1962 Big Joe Williams, after a number of successful recordings and two or three years of touring the universities, dropped out of sight and finally turned up playing five hours a night for $10, with a rough three piece

blues band in a colored dance hall in
St. Louis.

If in the blues there is an insistence
on infidelity and a rough sensuality it is
an imperfect reflection of the attitudes
of the entire Negro society, but it is a
direct response to the reality of the lives
of the singers and their audience.

The "love" that fills the blues has little of the sentimentality of the "love"
that dominates American popular song.
The love that is expressed in popular
song is an adolescent emotion, and the
words are filled with the vague yearn-
ings and misunderstandings of adolescent affairs. "Are you true?" "Can you
be true?" "Will you keep yourself true
to me?" There is a reiteration of the
theme that it is the heart that loves. "My
heart yearns for you," "I have given
you my heart," "You will live in my
heart." Instead of physical desire there
is ". . . the magic when we kiss," "My
heart stopped beating when you took
my hand," "I hold you in dreams . . ."
"Rest your head on my shoulder." It is
the painful, half understood awakening
of sexuality that is expressed, rather
than a love between adults. The kiss
becomes the physical expression of
love. "The lips you press to mine are
wet with tears," "I belong to you and

then we kiss," "I see you waiting there
for me with lips to kiss so tenderly,"
"Let me thrill to your kiss." Even the
awkwardness of a chance physical con-
tact is phrased in the language of the
kiss. "It is for you that my lips pucker
up when we dance to the music of the
band." The ideal of love is so distorted
that it is often years before the adolescent is able to reconcile his own experience with the unreal dream of love in
popular song. Some of them never are
able to outgrow it and there is a large
area of popular song which presents
the same distortion in an even more
grandiose form, usually with a sym-
phonic background and chorus. An
adult in American society who still
thinks of love in terms of his own popular song will find much of his emotional
experience disappointing and unsatis-
factory. The blues at least have the
strength of honesty, and, if there is
sometimes a lack of emotional subtlety
there is in the blues the expression of a
love that is mature and intensely felt.
In the blues there is an acceptance of
the reality of love, both physical and
emotional. As Pink Anderson sang in
the quiet back room of his small house
in Spartanburg, South Carolina,

*Well, that weeping willow, that
lonesome turtledove,*

*That weeping willow, lonesome turtle-
        dove,
Life isn't worth living if you're not with
        the one you love.*

Although the usual mood of the blues
is despondent, and it is misfortunes of
love that occupy the singer's mind,
there is an uninhibited joy in the de-
lights of love that runs through the
blues. A North Carolina singer, Blind
Boy Fuller, calls out to his woman,

*Hey mama! Hey girl!
Don't you hear me calling you?
You're so sweet, so sweet,
My baby, so sweet.*

*Say I love my baby, love her to her
        bone.
I hate to see my sweet sugar go home.
She's so sweet, so sweet,
My little woman, so sweet.*

*See my baby coming, don't get so
        smart.
I'll cut you just a little above your heart.
She's so sweet, so sweet,
My little woman, so sweet.*

*Hey mama! Hey girl!
Don't you hear Blind Boy Fuller calling
        you?*

You're so sweet, so sweet,
My little woman, so sweet.

Woman I love, she's done gone back
   home.
When I think I'm treating her right I
   must be doing wrong,
She's so sweet, so sweet,
My little woman, so sweet.

I make a million trips for robbing a little
   bee,
But the woman I love is sweeter than
   anything in this world to me.
She's so sweet, so sweet,
My little woman, so sweet.

Hey mama! Hey girl!
Don't you hear me calling you?
You're so sweet, so sweet,
My baby, so sweet.

Fuller means every word of it, even
if in another blues he could sing,

I never loved
  But a thousand womens in my life,
Oh Lord,
  But a thousand womens in my life.

He even insists that his love for his
newest woman is so strong that he

couldn't be interested in someone else,
that ". . . it can't be turned around."

Now the love I have for you, woman,
    God knows it sure is strong.
Oh Lord,
    God knows it sure is strong.

Then if you love me, woman,
    Then you won't do nothing wrong,
Oh Lord,
    And you won't do nothing wrong.

Now, my woman, please don't worry,
    Baby, while I'm out of your town,
Oh Lord,
    While I'm out of your town.

Now the love I have for you, woman,
    God knows it can't be turned
        around,
Oh Lord,
    And it can't be turned around . . .

In the many blues that Fuller wrote
celebrating the emotional and physical
joys of love he seems to have made
only one exception to the kind of
women that interested him. He was not
interested in women who were thin.

Little lean woman can't draw my pay.
She haven't got a thing to drive my
        blues away.
Little lean woman can't draw my pay.

*She haven't got nothing to drive my
blues away . . .*

There is also in the blues some of the
poignancy of the first awakening of
love. Henry Townsend remembers
hearing the blues when he was a young
man and in the singing of Lonnie Johnson he found some of what he was
experiencing himself.

*. . . He used to explain himself very
distinct to me, and—this will embarrass
me but I'm going to have to say it—at
that time I was trying life too, and I run
into the same things he was running
into; so I gathered what he was saying
had to be true.*

Townsend first recorded when he was
still in his late adolescence, and in one
of his blues he said plaintively,

*Baby, don't mistreat me because you
know I'm young and wild.
I said, Baby, don't mistreat me, 'cause
I am young and wild.
'Cause you must remember, baby, one
time you was a child.*

then he went on with the sudden con-
fidence of youth,

*But never mind, never mind, baby, I've
      got my eyes on you.*
*But it's never mind, never mind, baby,
      I've got my eyes on you.*
*And some old day, pretty baby, you'll
      do like I want you to do.*

And with youth's pride he went on in
another blues,

*That's all right for you, babe, I pawned
      my watch and ring.*
*For you, babe, pawned my watch and
      ring.*
*I done give you my money, I can give
      you most anything.*

Sometimes the mood of love is quiet
and restrained. There is an older verse
which is still used by many of the city
singers, among them Hociel Thomas.

*Today, today, today, been a long old
      lonesome day.*
*Today, today, today, have been a long
      old lonesome day.*
*I been sitting here thinking, with my
      mind a million miles away.*

Another of the women singers, Alice
Moore, remembered the physical torment of love.

*If you've ever lay down thinking about
your man at night.*
*If you've ever lay down thinking about
your man at night.*
*And he will get you twisting and
turning, and you couldn't lay just
right.*

There is another widely known verse
about sleepless nights, and Pink Anderson used it to tell his woman how important they were to each other.

*Now last night I lay down and I tried to
take my rest.*
*Last night I lay down and I tried to take
my rest.*
*And my mind started wandering like a
wild goose in the west.*

*I says, baby, you goin' need, you goin'
need my help someday.*
*Baby, you goin' need my help some-
day.*
*It might be here, baby, it may be miles
away.*

Often, in the haphazard pattern of
their lives, the men have found themselves without someone to love, and in
a blues sung nearly everywhere there
is a half-serious story of someone looking for a woman he could make his
own.

I was standing on the corner with my
     hat in my hand,
Standing on the corner with my hat in
     my hand.
Looking for a woman, didn't have no
     man.

I cried, "All you womens, please don't
     pass me by."
Cryin', "All you womens, please don't
     pass me by."
I won't quit you, woman, 'til the day I
     die.

I stood out in the cold last night, stood
     in the cold the night before.
I stood out in the cold last night, out the
     night before.
Couldn't find no woman put me out on
     her kindlin' floor.

I was looking for a woman she wants to
     work and settle down,
I was looking for a woman wants to
     work and settle down.
Looking for a woman, Lord, she can't be
     found.

The "kindlin' floor" is the floor of the
shed where kindling for the fire is kept,
and the man is complaining that he
couldn't even find a woman who would
let him sleep on the floor of her shed.

There is still a tenderness in many of the blues that the men have sung to their women, and even in his anger at their first quarrel Memphis Willie B. remembers the love he has for the woman he has brought in to the city to live with him.

I went way out in the country and got
    you, baby, you was way out in
    the woods.
I went way out in the country and got
    you, baby, you was way out in
    the woods.
You know I got sick of you telling me
    that country life was no good.

You start to leave here early in the
    morning, you don't come back 'til
    the break of day.
You start to leave here early in the
    morning, you don't come back 'til
    the break of day.
You keep doing that you going to drive
    my love away.

Lord, I don't want to hurt your feelings
    'bout the little things you do
    that's wrong.
I don't want to hurt your feelings 'bout
    the little things you do that's
    wrong.
You know if I scold you God knows I
    don't mean you no harm.

Lord, the reason I love you, you the
    onliest girl in this world.
Lord, the reason I love you, you the
    onliest girl in this world.
You know I went to the country and got
    you, raised you from a little
    country girl.

5

*You can always tell when your woman
        got another man,
You can always tell when your woman
        got another man,
Your meals ain't regular and your
        house ain't never clean . . .*

Love dominates the blues, but it is not the exultant love of Blind Boy Fuller's verse, or the hesitant sensitivity in Henry Townsend's. Love, in the blues, is,

*. . . the achin' heart disease,
Like consumption, killing me by
        degrees.*

Love is the dominant theme of the popular song of nearly every culture, and the blues, the popular song of the Negro in America, is as much concerned with it; but in the blues it is the pain rather than the promise of love that is repeated over and over again. The unhappiness of love is such a persistent theme in the blues that the attitude has even become part of the definition of the word. In Webster's Dictionary the blues is, "A type of song . . with melancholy words." It is an unhappiness that has been caused by infidelity or by separation, with infidelity as the most common theme. As J. D. Short expressed it,

Well the blues mostly come on account of women because there is so many fellows that is in love with different womens that they actual love, and the woman was dishonest, and he'd love her from his very heart and she'd get in love with somebody else and go away and leave him. So that would leave him weepin' and moanin', and then he would take hisself back to his room and he have got what you may call the blues, and he just try to sing to make hisself confident.

And as Ma Rainey sang,

*People have different blues and think
     they're mighty sad,
But blues about a man the worst I ever
     had . . .*

Sometimes, it is only the suspicion of infidelity,

*My man left me and he never said a
     word,
My man left me and he never said a
     word,*

*It wasn't nothing I did, it must have
      been something that he heard,*

a glimpse a man has caught of his
woman on the street,

*Uumh, woman, you don't do what you
      say,*
*Uumh, woman, you don't do what you
      say,*
*You say you love me, but what about
      the man I saw you with the other
      day.*

In sudden anger the man seizes his
woman and shouts,

*I want you to tell me, little girl, just
      where did you stay last night?*
*I want you to tell me, little girl, just
      where did you stay last night?*
*Your clothes is all wrinkled, and your
      shoes isn't tied up right.*

then he warns her,

*I feel like snapping my pistol in your
      face,*
*I feel like snapping my pistol in your
      face,*

*Let that cold iron grave be your resting
      place.*

Often a man goes out and tries to find
her. Blind Lemon Jefferson sang, in
"Pneumonia Blues," of a wet, rainy
night, when he tried to find where his
woman was staying.

*Slippin' 'roun' the corner, runnin' up
    alleys, too,
I went slippin' 'roun' the corner, runnin'
    up alleys, too.
Watchin' to see my woman, tryin' to
    see what she goin' to do.*

*Sit down in the street one cold dark
    stormy night,
I sat down in the street, one dark and
    stormy night.
Tryin' to see if my good girl, she goin'
    make it home all right.*

*I believe she's found something that
    probably made her fall.
She must did found something and I
    believe made her fall.
I stood out in the cold all night, and she
    didn't come home at all . . .*

Even when the man tries not to think
about what she might be doing he lies
in bed unable to sleep.

*It's four o'clock in the morning, and I
    can't close my eyes,*

*It's four o'clock in the morning, and I
      can't close my eyes,*
*I can't find my woman, I can't be
      satisfied.*

*I can't find her hat and clothes, I
      wonder where could they be.*
*I can't find her hat and clothes, I
      wonder where could they be.*
*I can't sleep for the evil thoughts that
      come over me.*

Finally he has to get up.

*I walked all night, I can't even take my
      rest.*
*I walked all night, I can't even take my
      rest.*
*You know I believe I love that woman,
      I love that gal the best.*

*I looked for that woman, between
      midnight and day,*
*I looked for that woman, between
      midnight and day,*
*Looking for my woman, trying to find
      where she stay.*

Sometimes he wanders the streets with
a pistol, trying to find the woman and
the man who has taken her from him.
One of the blues known by nearly
every singer is some variation of the
old "Forty-Four Blues," named for the

.44 caliber revolver that the man is
carrying with him. It is also a well-
known piano solo that most barrel-
house and boogie woogie men include
in their repertoire. The caliber of the
revolver keeps changing as smaller re-
volvers become popular, but the form
of the blues is still the same. James
Wiggins sang,

I walked all night long, with my .44 in
    my hand.
I walked all night long, with my .44 in
    my hand.
Looking for my woman, looking for her
    other man.

I was gone so long, running from store
    to store.
I was gone so long, running from store
    to store.
When I find my woman she won't run
    no more.

When I found that woman they was
    walking hand in hand.
When I found that woman they was
    walking hand in hand.
You know she did surprise me when I
    found her with another man.

She started screaming before I even
    raised my hand.

> She started screaming before I even
> raised my hand.
> She saw I was carrying my .44 in my
> hand.

In the 1920's it was a .44 or a .45 revolver, in the 1930's it had become a .38,
a .32, or a .32-.20, and by the 1950's it
was a .25 or a .22. Memphis Willie B.,
who had been a veteran, and brought
a German revolver back from Europe
with him, sang it as "P-.38 Blues."

Sometimes the suspicion of infidelity
is only a vague feeling that something
has happened to the relationship,

> You can always tell when your woman
> got another man,
> You can always tell when your woman
> got another man,
> Your meals ain't regular and your
> house ain't never clean,

or, as a woman would sing,

> You always know when you 'bout to
> lose your man,
> You always know when you 'bout to
> lose your man,
> Won't do nothin' for you, won't do the
> best he can.

but often the suspicion is stronger, as in
Memphis Willie B.'s bitterly vivid verse,

*Your clothes is wrinkled, little girl, your
        shade is pulled down low,
You know your clothes is wrinkled,
        little girl, and your shade is
        pulled down low.
There's a towel layin' 'cross the bed,
        and a pan of water on the floor.*

As he stands in the darkened room he
realizes that she has been in the arms
of another man.

Often, when the love is sincere, the
person in love asks only that any infidelity be kept from them. Clara Smith
sang,

*You can cheat on me, you can steal on
        me, you can fool me all along.
You can cheat on me, you can steal on
        me, you can fool me all along.
All I ask you, daddy, please don't let
        me catch you wrong,*

And a verse used by several blues men
repeats this attitude with a warning.

*I'm a hard-working man and, baby, I
        don't mind trying,
I'm a hard-working man and, baby, I
        don't mind trying,
I catch you cheating on me, then, baby,
        you don't mind dying.*

But more often there is just an awareness that the relationship is over. In

Alice Moore's "My Man Blues" she
uses the classic blues form. Something
has happened, which is the betrayal in
the last verse, and her first verses develop her mood as she thinks about her
unhappiness.

My man, my man, leaves me so low
    down,
My man, my man, leaves me so low
    down.
Everything I do, seems like to me is
    wrong.

I love my man, but he loves somebody
    else,
I love my man, but he loves somebody
    else,
I think I'm a damn fool to keep on
    worrying myself.

If you've ever lay down thinkin' about
    your man at night,
If you've ever lay down thinkin' about
    your man at night,
And he will get you twistin' and turnin'
    and you couldn't lay just right.

My baby came to me with the tears
    rolling down his face,
My baby came to me with the tears
    rolling down his face,
Babe, I'm sorry for you, but some other
    woman has taken your place.

For Charlie Lincoln it was coming
back to his cabin and finding that he
wasn't welcome.

When I came home this morning my
    wife she met me at the door,
When I came home this morning my
    wife she met me at the door,
"Go away, sweet daddy," she says, "I
    can't use you no more."

Hey, hey, mama, baby what's the
    matter now?
Hey, hey, mama, baby what's the
    matter now?
Say, you trying to quit me, honey, and
    you don't know how.

(Spoken) Yes, I know you been acting
    funny about a week or two.

Well it ain't no love, mama, sure ain't
    no getting along.
It ain't no love, sure ain't no getting
    along.
Say my brown treat me so mean that I
    don't know right from wrong.

Take me back, baby, try me just one
    more time,
Oh take me back, baby, try me one
    more time.
If I don't do to suit you I'll break my
    backbone trying . . .

Sometimes the women boasted about their affairs. In "Nickel's Worth of Liver" Edith Johnson sang,

*I got a man upstairs, one downstairs,
one across the street,
You got your eyes wide open, but
you're sound asleep,*

and in "Good Chib Blues" she didn't hesitate to tell her man that she could do just as well with anybody else.

*Uumh, tomorrow I may be far away.
Uumh, tomorrow I may be far away.
Don't try to drive me, honey, sweet talk
can't make me stay.*

*Now if you get loaded, baby, and think
you want to go,
Now if you get loaded, baby, and think
you want to go,
Remember, baby, you ain't no better
than the man I had before.*

*When I get drunk I'm evil, I don't know
what to do,
When I get drunk I'm evil, I don't know
what to do,
Guess I'll get some good chib and get
something good from you.*

*Now the man I love he's just about the
height of me,*

*Now the man I love he's just about the
      height of me,
I'm five feet two, Lord, and that sweet
      man's five feet three.*

Ida Cox insisted on the same freedom,
and even defended her attitude.

*. . . I've got a different system and a
      way of my own,
When my man starts kicking I let him
      find another home.
I get a full of good liquor and walk the
      street all night,
Go home and put my man out if he don't
      treat me right,
Wild women don't worry, wild women
      don't have the blues.*

*You never get nothing by being an
      angel child,
You better change your ways and get
      real wild.
I want to tell you something I wouldn't
      tell you no lie,
Wild women are the only kind that
      really get by,
'Cause wild women don't worry, wild
      women don't have the blues.*

Ida Cox is still living in Chicago, and
Mrs. Johnson lives in St. Louis, where
she still sings occasionally for friends.
They are both often startled when they

hear some of their old recordings, and Edith listens with an indulgent smile, shaking her head as she remarks, "That certainly is some woman that's talking there."

The men who knew that a woman was having an affair sometimes warned her about her young boyfriend, her "kid man," but as Pink Anderson said, it wasn't anybody's business.

Oh, woman, it ain't none of my
business,
But you know it sure ain't right.
Lay 'round with your kid man all day
And play sick on your husband at
night . . .
(Spoken) He love you, too.

The men talked about their infidelities even more than the women, sometimes boasting, sometimes complaining about the difficulties of meeting their women. There is a rich strain of poetry from the country singers who had to cross the fields at night and slip unnoticed into a littered back yard. The Mississippi singers use a verse which catches the moment when the man first sees his woman coming toward him as he stands in the shadows looking into the moonlight.

Don't the moon look pretty, shining
through the trees,

*I can see my woman, Lord, but she can't
    see me.*

It is a terse poetic image, but as it is
sung to a droned guitar accompaniment by the heavy voice of Charlie
Patton or Son House it has a strong
evocative power. The Georgia singer,
Blind Willie McTell, in a number of
blues, one of them the beautifully
named, "Mamma, T'ain't Long Fo'
Day," caught the moment of hesitation
when the man has come close to his
woman's house and is trying to wake
her without anyone else nearby hearing
him.

*Wake up, mama, turn your lamp down
    low,*
*Wake up, mama, turn your lamp down
    low,*
*Have you got the nerve to drive Papa
    McTell from your door . . .*

*Wake up, mama, don't you sleep so
    hard,*
*Wake up, mama, don't you sleep so
    hard,*
*Bar these blues walkin' all over your
    yard . . .*

The woman comes to the window, and
he leans against the side of the cabin,
whispering to her in the darkness,

*I wrote you a letter, mama, put it in
     your front yard,
I wrote you a letter, mama, put it in
     your front yard,
I would love to come to see you, but
     your good man's got me
     barred . . .*

*I got these blues, I'm not satisfied,
I got these blues, I'm not satisfied,
That's the reason why I stole away and
     cried . . .*

Then he feels the first stirring of the
morning wind, and he turns to leave.

*The big star fallin', mama, 'tain't long
     fo' day,
The big star fallin', mama, 'tain't long
     fo' day,
Maybe the sunshine will drive these
     blues away . . .*

A man meets a woman on the road
and he has a chance to warn her that
he'll be coming to see her that night,

*I'm coming in your back yard, I'm
     coming one more time tonight.
I'm coming in your back yard, I'm
     coming one more time tonight.
Keep your dogs on a chain, mama,
     don't let your bulldog bite.*

Mississippi Bracey laughs when his woman tries to warn him about her husband,

*You got a bad husband now, baby, that
    will be alright,
You got a bad husband now, baby, that
    will be alright.
I will dodge your husband like a rabbit
    dodge a dog at night.*

Willie McTell even suggests that the uneasiness of jealousy still persists when he and his woman have finally fallen asleep in each other's arms.

*Don't get mad with me if I talk in my
    sleep,
Don't get mad with me if I talk in my
    sleep,
'Cause I might say something, good
    girl, to cause you to weep.*

*If you talk in your sleep, woman, don't
    you mention my name,
If you talk in your sleep, woman, don't
    you mention my name,
'Cause if you do you might drive my
    heart insane.*

In his "Mean Jumper Blues" Blind Lemon Johnson sketches out, in a beautifully controlled blues, the angry determination of a man to see a woman he

still loves, the lengthy story compressed
into five verses that move, with a careful inner logic, from his angry frustration to his nearly tragic meeting with
the woman's new lover.

*I feel like jumping through the keyhole
in your door.*
*I feel like jumping through the keyhole
in your door.*
*If you jump this time, baby, you won't
jump no more.*

He is telling her that if she'll "jump"
to him she won't want to go on to another man.

*I feel like falling from a treetop to the
ground.*
*I feel like falling from a treetop to the
ground.*
*My rider's got a mean joker, and he
don't 'low me 'round.*

"Rider" and its longer term "Easy
Rider" is meant as a reference to their
sexual relationship.

*I go there early in the morning, and I
goes there late at night.*
*I go there early in the morning, and I
goes there late at night.*
*Don't care how late I goes there he
have never turned out the light.*

Pink Anderson and son

Furry Lewis

Otis Spann

Muddy Waters *(left)*
Sleepy John Estes *(lower left)*
Henry Townsend *(lower right)*

Memphis Willie B.,
Furry Lewis, and
Gus Cannon *(facing)*

Robert Pete Williams
and Robert Wilkins (*facing*)

Mississippi John Hurt
and Skip James (*top*)
Sleepy John Estes, Yank
Rachel, and Hammie
Nixon (*above*)
J. D. Short (*right*)

Baby Tate

*I believe he's looking for me; he's up all
        hours at night.*
*I believe he's looking for me; he's up all
        hours at night.*
*She used to be my rider, and he ain't
        treating her right.*

He is complaining about the way the
new man is acting toward the woman,
but in the final verse he seems to be
afraid to do anything for her.

*I met this joker one morning, and he
        was out on the edge of town.*
*I met this joker one morning, and he
        was out on the edge of town.*
*I had to talk and plead to keep him
        from blowing me down.*

One of the most poetic of the images
describing infidelity is the "fo' day
creep," and it is often used by city singers. It describes the sounds of someone
leaving a room just before the first light
of morning. As Black Ace sings it, it
becomes a bitter social commentary.

*It was early this morning, I was 'bout
        half asleep.*
*I heard somebody making a 'fore day
        creep.*
*What's that I hear in the morning so
        soon?*

*Something sound mighty funny, baby,
    in the next room.*

*I heard a low whisper, the door begin
    to cry,
It wasn't the milkman, 'cause he done
    passed on by.
What's that I hear in the morning so
    soon?
Something sound mighty funny, baby,
    in the next room.*

*He don't know and he never will,
The child she got ain't none of his.
What's that I hear in the morning so
    soon?
Something sound mighty funny, baby,
    in the next room.*

*It ain't my business, but I know it ain't
    right,
But that's what happen to a man that
    works at night.
What's that I hear in the morning so
    soon?
Something sound mighty funny, baby,
    in the next room.*

There is little concern with conventional morality in the blues. The attitude
toward marriage and fidelity is not hyp-
ocritical, as in the popular song of the
larger American society. While the
popular song remains in its adolescent

dream of unending tremulous affection,
the blues, with a complete frankness,
accepts the reality of adultery and
promiscuity with a resigned shrug. The
honesty of the expression is so complete
that it is futile to argue with the moral
value implied. Infidelity is a common
experience, although this makes it no
less painful when it happens. Sleepy
John Estes sings, without hesitation,

I asked sweet mama, let me be her kid,
She said, "I might, but I like to keep it
  hid."
Well, she looked at me, she begin to
  smile,
Says, "I thought I would use you for my
  man awhile,
Just don't let my husband
  Catch you here,
Just don't let my husband
  Catch you here."

In another blues he frankly sings about
his affairs with other men's wives.

Now don't never take a married woman
  to be your friend,
She will get all of your money, take the
  same man back again.

Now a married woman, she always
  been my crave.

*Now a married woman, she always
been my crave.*
*Now a married woman want to carry
me to my grave.*

*Now just as sure as the grass on this
earth grows green,*
*Now just as sure as the grass on this
earth grows green,*
*I ain't crazy 'bout no woman that I ever
seen.*

In one of his finest blues, "When You Fall For Someone That's Not Your Own," Lonnie Johnson described the troubled emotions of someone involved in an adulterous relationship, and with a despairing honesty sang about the pain of his own woman's unfaithfulness. He found that even his own adultery was painful to him, since he couldn't help being jealous of the woman's husband.

*You tell me you've had trouble and
worry all of your life.*
*You tell me you've had trouble and
worry all of your life.*
*Man, but you ain't had no trouble 'til
you fall for a married man's wife.*

*When it begin raining and you looking
through your windowpane,*

When it begin raining and you looking
      through your windowpane,
And crazy about another man's wife,
      it's enough to drive you insane.

But a married woman's sweet, the
      sweetest woman ever was born.
A married woman's sweet, the sweetest
      woman ever was born,
Only thing that hurts you she have to
      go home sometime.

The poetic image of his standing at
the window looking into the rain is very
moving, and there is a sadness to the
blues. He realized that if he were to
have an affair with someone else's
wife he couldn't expect anything different from his own. He sang,

They tell me blues and trouble walk
      hand in hand.
They tell me blues and trouble walk
      hand in hand.
But you ain't had no trouble 'til your
      woman falls for some no good
      man.

A married woman will swear she'll love
      you all of her life.
A married woman will swear she'll love
      you all of her life.
And meet her other man around the
      corner and tell that same lie
      twice.

Then if you get a woman of your own
and make her happy night and
day,
Then if you get a woman of your own
and make her happy night and
day,
There will be some no good man she'll
fall for, pretty soon she'll go
away.

There is a verse sung by nearly every blues singer which comments on the infidelity that is part of their rough and haphazard lives, and there is an angry edge to the words.

A nickel is a nickel, a dime is a dime,
I got a house full of children, ain't none
of them mine,
Yes, a nickel is a nickel, Lord, a dime is
a dime.
I got a house full of children, Lord, ain't
none of them mine.

Blind Lemon Jefferson described a confrontation between a man and a woman over the treatment she is giving a child.

Well, she grabbed my baby and
spanked him, and I tried to make
her leave him alone.
Well, she grabbed my baby and
spanked him, and I tried to make
her leave him alone.

*I tried my best to stop her, but she said
      the baby ain't none of mine.*

His final comment was a cynical shrug.

*The woman rocks the cradle, I declare
      she rules the home.
Woman rocks the cradle, I declare she
      rules the home.
Many a man rocks some other man's
      baby, and the fool thinks he's
      rocking his own.*

When it was finally obvious that the love was "in vain," and that the person that they were living with was being unfaithful, then there had to be a separation. Sometimes there was violence. Billie Pierce turns her tired face from the piano, her eyes closed as she sings,

*If you know you did not want me,
      daddy, you had no right to lie.
If you know you did not want me,
      daddy, you had no right to lie.
'Cause the day you quit me, daddy,
      that's the day you going to die.*

If his woman was unfaithful a man could throw her out of the house. Sleepy John Estes, who could describe asking another man's wife to be her "kid," shouts at his own woman after she has been unfaithful,

Now drop down, baby, let your daddy
be,
I know jus' what you're trying to pull
on me.
Well, my ma, she don't 'low me to fool
roun' all night long.
Now I may look like I'm crazy, but poor
John do know right from wrong.

He is telling her to go away and let
him alone. His mother doesn't allow
him to stay out all night, and does this
woman think he doesn't know that what
she's doing is wrong?

Go 'way from my window, quit
scratching on my screen,
You's a dirty mistreater, I know just
what you mean.
Well, my ma, she don't 'low me to fool
roun' all night long.
Now I may look like I'm crazy, but poor
John do know right from wrong.

Then he adds petulantly,

Some of these women sure do make me
tired,
Got a handful of "gimme" and a
mouthful of "much obliged."
Well, my ma, she don't 'low me to fool
roun' all night long.
Now I may look like I'm crazy, but poor
John do know right from wrong.

Sometimes the mood is quiet and resigned, and Clara Smith summed up
her attitude in one thoughtful line.

If nobody wanted him, neither would I.

As she expressed it in a verse,

If you take my daddy, take my daddy,
  I hope you be kind and true.
If you take my daddy, take my daddy,
  I hope you be kind and true.
Just like you took him from me, some-
  body's sure to take him from
  you.

There is a country expression, "fatten-
ing frogs for snake," and in the blues it
means that a woman has been taking
care of a man until another woman has
found him interesting enough to steal.
If his woman left him, Skip James could
sing with a casual shake of the head,

Woman I love,
Woman I love,
Woman I love,
Stole her from my best friend.
That joker got lucky, stole her back
  again.

If the love has ended; then the relationship can end without bitterness or
aggravation. There is a common verse

expressing the thoughts of a man and a
woman as they stand together for a last
moment, trying to think of something to
say.

> I'm leaving now, let's shake hand in
>   hand.
> I'm leaving now, let's shake hand in
>   hand.
> I'm going to find me another woman,
>   you better find you another man.

6

In a ragged work song verse that was heard by an early collector of Negro songs in the fields outside of Auburn, Alabama, there is already a suggestion of another of the dominant themes in the poetry of the blues.

When a woman takes the blues
She tucks her head and cries.
But when a man catches the blues,
He catches a freight and rides.

The pain of separation and loneliness is as much a part of the blues as the pain of promiscuity and infidelity. As the early blues singers moved from town to town, stopping for a few weeks to work at a laboring job or to sing in a local dance hall, they left their women behind them, sometimes thinking about them as they went down the road, but usually forgetting them when they'd gotten to a new town and found someone new to take care of their worries. The women were left with " . . . an awful achin' head, lying in my empty bed," a few memories and empty nights

until they could find another man. The
blues singers drifted from work gang
to work gang, the men working beside
them as lonely as they were. In the poverty and discrimination of the South
were strong forces moving them on,
forcing them from one poorly paid job
to another, forcing them to leave towns
where they'd said the wrong thing or
gotten into trouble with a boss or a
storekeeper. Along the dirt roads and
the railroad tracks men moved from the
levee camps to the road gangs, from
the mills of towns like Birmingham to
the docks of ports like Mobile or Savan-
nah. They slept in sheds, beside the
roads, in ramshackle rooms above
noisy country saloons, in "hobo jungles" beside the railroad, sometimes
singing in the streets to earn a little
money. But as Blind Lemon Jefferson
commented,

I stood on the corner and almost bust
        my head,
I stood on the corner and almost bust
        my head.
I couldn't earn enough money to buy
        me a loaf of bread.

Strung along the meandering roads
or in the ugly "nigger towns" which the
South has left on the edges of its towns
and cities are men and women who

have no opportunity to leave. They are
tied to the land in a ruinous share-crop
arrangement or they have found a job
which offers them at least a little se-
curity. But the men and woman around
them swell the stream of people who
move with a driven restlessness. Despite the violent efforts that were made
to force them to stay in the South hundreds of thousands of Negroes fled to
the North. Men went alone to try to find
a job. Women left to try to find relatives
or someone they had loved. Families
moved from their lonely cabins, riding
to the North in the crowded "jim crow"
cars that the railroad permitted them to
use, usually worn and shabby train
equipment without provisions for food
or sleeping. Between 1950 and 1960
nearly 325,000 Negroes fled the state of
Mississippi, and over 220,000 fled the
state of Alabama. In the restlessness of
the men who moved from job to job, in
the instability of the life at this lowest
edge of society, in the forced emigra-
tion from the South, in each of these is
an emotional force which has produced
some of the most intense blues poetry.

Often the anger and frustration that
they found in the life they were forced
to lead intensified the rootlessness of
the singers. One of the oldest blues

verses, one known throughout the South, says simply,

Feeling tomorrow, like I feel today.
If I feel tomorrow, like I feel today,
I'll pack my suitcase, make my get
      away.

For the woman there was little she could do but try to forget that someday her man would wake up and ask her to " . . . reach in the corner, hand me my traveling shoes." The experience which Ma Rainey described was sung over and over again in the blues.

My man left this morning just about
      half past four.
My man left this morning just about
      half past four.
He left a note on the pillow saying he
      couldn't use me no more.

I grabbed my pillow, turned over in my
      bed.
I grabbed my pillow, turned over in my
      bed.
I cried about my daddy until my cheeks
      turned cherry red.

It's awful hard to take it, it was such a
      bitter pill.
It's awful hard to take it, it was such a
      bitter pill.

*If the blues don't kill me that man's
      meanness will . . .*

The women were just as free to leave,
and often their restlessness would lead
them to another man, or just on to
another poorly paid job in another
lonely town. Her man was left to get
over it as best he could. In "Lonesome
Atlanta Blues," Bobby Grant sang of his
unhappiness and for a moment decided
to try to find where his woman had
gone.

I'm so lonesome,
God, so lonesome,
Hear me cryin',
Baby, I ain't lyin',
I'm so lonesome, got those lonesome
        Atlanta Blues,
I'm so sad and lonesome, mama, don't
        know what to do.

I'm going to walk down that dirt road,
That long, long dirt road,
That dirty old dirt road,
That darn old dirt road.
I'm going to walk down that dirt road
        'til somebody lets me ride.
If I can't find my baby, I'll run away
        and hide.

But as he went on, ruefully, it was
usually better just to separate.

*If you ever have the feeling that your
    gal don't want you no mo',
If you ever have the feeling that your
    gal don't want you no mo',
You might as well leave her, even if it
    hurts you so.*

They even sang about the highways
they had to travel, and there are several blues like Big Joe Williams' "Highway 49," Tommy McClennan's "Highway 51," and Charlie Pickett's "Down
The Highway." Most of them were
about Mississippi highways. U. S. 49
runs from the Gulf coast between Bi-
loxi and Gulfport to Jackson, Mississippi; then divides into 49 East and 49
West through the delta, stopping near
the Mississippi River at Clarksdale.
U. S. 51 goes through the heart of Mississippi, from New Orleans in the south
to Memphis in the north, crossing U. S.
49 just outside of Jackson. Charlie Pickett's "Down The Highway," is about the
river road, U. S. 61. It meanders along
the Mississippi's bank, through the flat,
hot cotton land of the delta to Clarksdale and Memphis. Memphis Willie B.
used 61 for his highway blues, and in
it are many of the themes of loneliness
and anger that fill these songs of root-
less wandering. Its third verse, " . . . I'm
going to travel 61 by myself, So's I get
killed on my journey no one will know

my death," is one of his most bitter
statements.

I'm going to leave here walking, going
     down highway 61.
I'm going to leave here walking, going
     down highway 61.
If I run up on my no good Joanie I
     declare we'll have some fun.

Oh yes, I'm going to make everything
     all right.
Oh yes, I'm going to make everything
     all right.
If I don't today, baby, says I will
     tomorrow night.

I says I'm leaving in the morning, I'm
     going to travel 61 by myself,
I says I'm leaving in the morning, I'm
     going to travel 61 by myself,
So's I get killed on my journey no one
     will know my death.

Fare you well, fare you well, to the state
     of old Tennessee.
Fare you well, fare you well, to the state
     of old Tennessee.
Say I'm going back to my no good
     Joanie, 'cause she won't come
     back to me.

Goodbye, baby, I ain't got no more to
     say.

> Goodbye, baby, I ain't got no more to
> say.
> Say I'll see you on 61 highway some
> dark and rainy day.

The train is a persistent image in
these restless blues, for much of the
longer traveling in the South was done
by train. There has been some change
in a few of the songs, since the Greyhound Bus lines are used as much now
as the trains. McClennan's image of
" . . . the Greyhound with his tongue
hangin' out on the side," is one of the
best known, and Robert Johnson, in
"Me And The Devil," sang,

> You can bury my body, down by the
> highway side.
> Lord, my old evil spirit can catch a
> Greyhound bus and ride.

But as the language of the blues has
become more fixed, with a growing
body of verses that have become almost
traditional, the tendency has grown to
use the older verses, even if they no
longer have direct relevance, just as
poets in other cultures use certain
words and phrases over and over. It is
still the train which ". . . took my baby
away," even though there is a great
deal more travel by bus and by car.
Singers still sing that they're going to

be with their woman " . . . if they have
to ride the rods," but there hasn't been a
freight car with "rods," the metal rein-
forcements under freight cars built at
the end of the 19th century, on a railroad for the last twenty years, and those
were only older equipment that had
been pressed into service during the
war. Already a conscious "artistic" attitude has become part of the blues, if
only on the level of a sentimentality for
trains, which would probably suprise
most of the singers if they stopped to
think about it.

When the idiom of the blues was developing, however, the train still was
the most common form of transporta-
tion, and young Charlie McCoy, accompanying himself with an agitated
rhythm on his mandolin, complained, in
"That Lonesome Train Took My Baby
Away."

*Woke up this morning, found something
        wrong,*
*My loving baby had caught that train
        and gone.*
*Now won't you starch my jumper, iron
        my overalls.*
*I'm going to ride that train that they call
        the "Cannonball."*

Depot Agent, close your depot down.

> The woman I'm loving she's fixin' to
> blow this town.
> Now that mean old fireman, that cruel
> old engineer,
> Gonna take my baby and leave me
> lonesome here.

> It ain't no telling what that train won't
> do.
> It'll take your baby and run right over
> you.
> Now that engineer man ought to be
> 'shamed of hisself,
> Take women from their husbands,
> babies from their mothers'
> breasts.

> I walked down the track and the stars
> refused to shine,
> I looked like every minute I was going
> to lose my mind.
> Now my knees was weak, my footsteps
> was all awry,
> Now it looked like every minute I was
> stumbling under the way.

The verses have a strong emotional effect that is largely due to the details he has included. He asks somebody to get his clothes ready for him to " . . . starch my jumper, iron my overalls," then when he gets to the station he becomes angry with the engineer and the fireman for running the train. He can't find his woman and he has to take his anger out on someone; so he goes down the track after the train shouting angrily at them, so upset that he can hardly keep on his feet.

Noah Lewis, in a blues that he recorded with John Estes and Yank Rachel accompanying him, used the same image of asking the depot agent to help prevent his woman from leaving town. In "Ticket Agent Blues," he sang,

Depot Agent, turn your depot,
Turn your depot,
Turn your depot,
Depot Agent, please turn your depot
      roun'.
My woman's quit me, going to leave
      your town.

Sometimes the women could boast of leaving. Billie Pierce included two well-known verses in one of her blues performances.

When you see your woman coming,
      raise your window high,
When you see your woman coming,
      raise your window high.
When you see me leaving, hang your
      head and cry . . .

*I'm leaving you, daddy, I ain't coming
    back no more.*
*I'm leaving you, daddy, I ain't coming
    back no more.*
*When you see me leaving, hang black
    crepe on your door.*

The men, too, could talk casually of
leaving town. Henry Thomas, using an
archaic blues form, sings of going back
to say goodbye.

*I'm going away, babe, and it won't be
    long,*
*I'm going away, babe, and it won't be
    long,*
*I'm going away, babe, and it won't be
    long.*

Thomas was an older musician from
Texas, and in his blues were many of
the older verse styles.

*Just soon as that train leaves out of that
    Mobile Yard,*
*Just soon as that train leaves out of that
    Mobile Yard,*
*Just soon as that train leaves out of that
    Mobile Yard.*

*Come shake your hand, tell your father
    goodbye,*
*Come shake your hand, tell your father
    goodbye,*

*Come shake your hand, tell your father
    goodbye.*

He has had difficulty fitting the line
into the rhythm. He is telling her that he
has come to shake her hand and tell
her father goodbye.

In its best-known form the blues that
is concerned with a woman's departure
on the train mentions that the man
knows that she's leaving, and sometimes he even comes to the station with
her. There is still love between them,
but the woman has to leave. Pink
Anderson sang,

*My baby left me this morning, and she
    caught that Southern train.*
*My baby left me this morning, and she
    caught that Southern train,*
*When she got on board, that almost
    addled my brain.*

Uumh, I could hear that whistle blow.
Uumh, I could hear that whistle blow.
*Well, she blowed just like she ain't
    goin' to blow no more.*

Black Ace even remembered the train
that his woman left on.

*That Santa Fe took my baby December
    Ninth, Tuesday evening right
    around six.*

*That Santa Fe took my baby December
Ninth, Tuesday evening right
around six.
We didn't have no trouble, just didn't
have my business fixed.*

*I stood and looked at that train until it
went around the bend,
I stood and looked at that train until it
went around the bend.
I say, wonder will my baby ever think
of me again.*

*Well, it blowed just like, oh Lord, it
never blowed before.
Well, it blowed just like, oh Lord, it
never blowed before.
I saw my baby leaving, not to come
back no more . . .*

The train whistle has become a
mournful echo of his own unhappiness.
Henry Townsend describes the scene in
the station, trying to keep from crying
as his woman gets on board the train
that will take her away from him.

*Train is coming. I heard it coming
around the bend.
Train is coming. I heard it coming
around the bend.
It will take away my baby, I may never
see her face again.*

*When it pulled up to the station, and my
baby got on board;*
*When it pulled up to the station, and my
baby got on board;*
*My heart felt really heavy, it really was
a heavy load.*

*When she got on board I done fairly
well,*
*When she got on board I done fairly
well,*
*But when the driver wheels turn over
then my poor heart begins to
swell.*

*I heard the engineer blow the whistle,
and the fireman he rung the bell.*
*I heard the engineer blow the whistle,
and the fireman he rung the bell.*
*I know there was a long goodbye when
she waved her hand farewell.*

*Why did she leave me, people, I really
would like to know.*
*Why did she leave me, people, I really
would like to know.*
*I would like somebody to tell me why
did my baby have to go.*

Even if there was an emotional sta-
bility in his life the singer often found
himself moving from job to job to try
to make some sort of living. Big Joe
Williams grew up on a farm in northern

Mississippi, but he couldn't see anything in the farm except a lifetime of endless labor; so he wandered along the levee camps and the pine camps in the Mississippi delta.

Yes, when I first started traveling, took
    the delta to be my home.
Yes, when I first started traveling, took
    the delta to be my home.
Yes, when I got to Greenville,
    Mississippi, all I could do hang
    my head and moan.

Uumh, ain't goin' cry no more.
Uumh, ain't goin' cry no more.
Old Joe getting old, Big Joe getting old.

When I walked to Crawford,
    Mississippi, Moorehead ain't my
    home.
Yes, I walked to Crawford, Mississippi,
    Moorehead ain't my doggone
    home.
Tell me the delta, oh Lord, that be my
    baby's home.

When I first started traveling, took the
    delta to be my home.
When I first started traveling, took the
    delta to be my home.
I left my woman there, somebody's
    done me wrong.

Some of the most interesting blues
about traveling were written by Sleepy
John Estes, who lived outside of Brownsville, Tennessee, but did much of his
recording in Chicago. Sometimes he
traveled by car, but it was an automobile accident that caused the near
drowning that he described in "Floating
Bridge," and on several trips he hopped
freights. John has always been interested in the literal details of anything
that has happened to him, and his
travel blues have a delightful sponta-
neity, even when they are warning
other men to watch out for railroad police and the Brownsville sheriff. He was
singing about the late 1920's and the
early 1930's, when the depression had
swelled the numbers of men who were
riding the freights and sleeping in the
hobo jungles, as in his blues, "Hobo
Jungle."

Now, when I left Chicago, I left on that
    G & M.
Now, when I left Chicago, I left on that
    G & M.
Then after I reach my home I have to
    change over on that L & N.

Now, when I came in on the main west
    I put it down at Chicago height.
Now, when I came in on the main west
    I put it down at Chicago height.

> *Now you know the hobo jungle and*
> *that's where I stayed the night.*
>
> *Now, if you hobo through Brownsville,*
> *you better not be peeping out.*
> *Now, if you hobo through Brownsville,*
> *you better not be peeping out.*
> *Now Mr. Whitney will get you, and Mr.*
> *Guy Hare will wear you out.*
>
> *Now out east from Brownsville, about*
> *four miles from town.*
> *Now out east from Brownsville, about*
> *four miles from town.*
> *If you ain't got your fare that's where*
> *they will let you down.*

In the poetry of Estes' blues there is an artless sincerity that is often very touching. By "peeping out" he means looking out through the partly open box car doors as the train slowly passes through the southern end of the small town. In another blues that he wrote about traveling he described a trip out of Ripley, Tennessee, which is a small town to the west of Brownsville on the mainline from Memphis to Chicago. As he hides in the boxcar he can hear the railroad detective, the "special agent," walking along the wooden catwalk on the roof of the car. As he says, some of the railroad police were brutal toward anyone they caught, but he only asks

that if he does get put off the train,
would they drop him near a town, since
he's already late for his recording date.

Now, when I left old Ripley the weather
      was kind of cool.
Now, when I left old Ripley the weather
      was kind of cool.
Say, boy, you'll be careful, you might
      catch the flu.

Now, I swung that 97, I went down in
      three rail stops.
Now, I swung that 97, I went down in
      three rail stops.
I could hear the special agent when he
      comes tippin' over the top.

He seems to mean that he got from
Ripley to Memphis in three stops. The
special agent was "tippin'," an expression for tiptoeing. Estes did a great deal
of recording in Memphis before he began making his Chicago trips.

Now, some special agents up the
      country, they sure is hard on a
      man.
Now, some special agents up the
      country, they sure is hard on a
      man.
They will put him off when he's hungry
      and won't even let him ride no
      train.

> *Now, I was sitting down in Centralia,*
> *and I was sure was feeling bad.*
> *Now, I was sitting down in Centralia,*
> *and I was sure was feeling bad.*
> *Now, they wouldn't let me ride no fast*
> *train. Put me off the doggone*
> *train.*

> *Now, special agent, special agent, put*
> *me off close to some town.*
> *Now, special agent, special agent, put*
> *me off close to some town.*
> *Now, I got to do some recording, I ought*
> *to be recording right now.*

There has been another reason for
travel for hundreds of thousands of
younger Negroes in the United States.
Even though they had been deprived of
nearly every other right of full citizen-
ship they were not deprived of the right
to be drafted into the armed services,
and their experiences became part of
the blues as men found themselves in
training camps and in combat areas
everywhere in the world in both world
wars. There are still verses sung which
refer to the embarkations from Newport
News, Virginia, in 1918, most of them
beginning,

> *I'm going to Newport News, baby,*
> *take a battleship across the*
> *sea . . .*

and there were a number of richly detailed blues written during the second World War. Memphis Willie B. was drafted in January, 1942, and in December, 1942, took part in the invasion of North Africa. He took part in later landings in Sicily and Italy, and in April, 1945, when Germany surrendered he was with a Quartermaster unit in the mountains in northern Italy. It was rumored that men were to be transferred from the European front to the war that was still raging in the Pacific, and after nearly two and a half years of combat Willie B. had had enough. He described the situation in his "Overseas Blues."

I was 'way overseas,
I was way over in New Jerusalem.
General Eisenhower said, "You soldiers
    got to go over to Tokyo,
And do the best you can."
But I told him, no, little Willie don't
    want to go.
Said I had so much trouble with the
    Germans,
Don't send me over in Tokyo.

He said, "Germany done fell now,
You soldier boys know what it's all
    about.
You go way over to the other islands,
And help General MacArthur out."

I told him, no, little Willie don't want to
    go.
I had so much trouble with the
    Germans,
Don't send me over in Tokyo.

You know General Eisenhower and
    General MacArthur had a
    conference.
They were talking about that atomic
    bomb.
He said, "Do whatever you think with
    the bomb;
So men won't have to come."
I said, no, little Willie don't want to go.
Said I had so much trouble with the
    Germans,
Don't send me over in Tokyo.

We was sitting in the stationary,
Waiting on the results of that atomic
    bomb.
Finally General Eisenhower and
    General MacArthur send a letter,
"You boys don't have to come."
I'm so glad, little Willie don't have to
    go.
Said I had so much trouble with the
    Germans,
Don't send me over in Tokyo.

I told them I had a sweet thing in the
    U. S. A.
She's as sweet as she can be.

She's got a lot of work she need did,
And she savin' the job for me.
That's why I'm crying, no, little Willie
        don't want to go.
I had so much trouble with the
        Germans,
Don't send me over in Tokyo.

7

It is often in its colorful and elaborate sexual imagery that the blues is most vividly poetic. There is a sauntering flamboyance to the language, a sudden image in one verse crowding into the next, its intended effect broadened with the tone of the voice or the rhythm of the guitar or piano. An exuberant, gusty delight in sexuality is expressed in an imagery which still has the vigor and freshness of its folk roots. Instead of the reticence or the leering innuendo of American popular song there is in the blues an open acceptance of the pleasure of sexual love. A singer may be more intensely emotional in a blues that bares his pain at separation or infidelity, but often in his erotic blues there will be a more brilliant virtuosity of language and style. There are many verses which have a directness and clarity of meaning,

Pull down your shade, mama, turn your
        lamp down low.
Pull down your shade, mama, turn your
        lamp down low.

*Then give me a last kiss, just before we
go.*

but usually there is a more imaginative
use of language.

*Um—um, black snake crawling in my
room.
Um—um, black snake crawling in my
room.
Yes, some pretty mama better get this
black snake soon.*

Some of the more vivid expressions
have even become part of the popular
vocabulary, but American society usually thinks of sex with either fright or a
nervous vulgarity. There is little open
acceptance of eroticism. When a sexual
expression passes from Negro to white
there is usually considerable confusion
over it. "Jazz" was one of the first expressions to become widely used. It had
several original meanings, but all of
them were sexual, and when Chicago
musicians called the first New Orleans
band to come north a "jass" band they
meant it as a ribald insult. In the 1930's
the expression "in the groove" became
popular, with its obvious reference to a
man's delight as he joins a woman, as
he " . . . gets in the groove," but its
meaning quickly was obscured, probably because many Negroes weren't in-

clined to explain it to anyone. It passed from one community to the other through one of the few points of exchange, music, and since musicians were using it the term took on musical implications. Webster's Dictionary now defines it as "Playing swing music in exalted mood." Even more recently the term "rock and roll" has become part of common usage. The term, of course, refers to the motions of the sexual embrace, but it crossed over, like "in the groove," through music. A fast blues style popular in the 1940's which was known to Negro musicians as "rhythm and blues," often used lyrics that included the terms "to rock" and "to roll." An early blues had used both expressions. "My daddy rocks me with one steady roll." The young white dancers who heard the music simply picked up the term without understanding it, and the future definitions of both words, "rock" and "roll" will probably have something to do with dancing. It is surprising to realize that the larger American society is so self-conscious about sexual love that even if it begins to use a sexual term it almost immediately alters its meaning so that it becomes no longer sexual.

The blues have little of this reticence. There is an exultant eroticism even in

the titles of many of the blues recordings. Intercourse is frankly described in
titles like "She Moves It Just Right,"
"I'm Wild About That Thing," "I'm Going To Have It Now," "Warm It Up To
Me," "Do It A Long Time," "Slow Driving," "Drive It Down," and even in an
instrumental solo the great blues trom-
bonist Ike Rogers was able to express
an intense sexuality in a piece he called
"It Hurts So Good." Sometimes the
imagery is intentionally humorous. "My
Banana In Your Fruit Basket," "My Pin
In Your Cushion," or "I Want Some Of
Your Pie." The masculine erection is
referred to in blues like "Ramrod Daddy," and "Hard Pushing Papa"; the men
asking the women "Let Me Be Your
Stem Winder," "Let Me Scoop For You,"
or "Let Me In Your Saddle." Sometimes
they even complained. "You've Had
Too Much," "The Stuff You Sell Ain't No
Good," "My Pencil Won't Write No
More." The women sang blues about
the "black snake" and the "sweet potato," the "stingaree." The men sang
about the "jelly roll" and the "sweet
honey hole." As Jim Jackson put it, in a
line he used in two or three of his blues,

If you want to be a woman of mine,
        you've got to bring it with you
    when you come . . .

There is such a directness of expression in the sexual attitudes of the blues that there is even occasional mention of both homosexuality and lesbianism. The high-voiced George Hannah sang,

Called me a freakish man, what more
    was there to do.
She called me a freakish man, what
    more was there to do.
Just because she said I was strange
    that did not make it true.

You mix ink with water, bound to turn
    it black.
You mix ink with water, bound to turn
    it black.
You run around with funny people you
    get a streak of it up your back.

There was a time when I was alone, my
    freakish way to treat,
There was a time when I was alone, my
    freakish way to treat,
But they're so common now you get one
    every day in the week.

Had a strange feeling this morning,
    where I've had it all day.
Had a strange feeling this morning,
    where I've had it all day.
I wake up one of these mornings that
    feeling will be here to stay.

and Memphis Willie B. complained,

Women loving each other, they don't
    think about no man.
Women loving each other, they don't
    think about no man.
They ain't playing it secret no more.
    These women playing a wide-
    open hand.

I buzzed a girl the other day,
I wanted a little thrill,
She said, "I'm so sorry,
My missus is putting out the
    same thing you is,"
Women loving each other, they don't
    think about no man.

They ain't playing it secret no more.
    These women playing a wide-
    open hand.

but the sexual expression of the blues is usually concerned with the heterosexual relationship.

The poetic language of the sexual blues uses a rich and often highly imaginative imagery. It has the enduring persistence of a folk idiom, and it is part of the repertoire of every singer. There is another area of sexual blues, however, which reflect some of the attitudes of the larger society. It has always been evident that sexual blues could be commercially successful, and there have been occasional efforts made by the record companies to exploit this material. Most of the records which were produced with this in mind used the cheapened styles of the party records which have a large illicit sale in the white society. They relied on an uncomfortable suggestiveness, the point usually being that the entire record, which is made as suggestive as possible, is really not about sex, but about something which can be described in terms that can be interpreted as sexual. It has little relationship to an acceptance of physical love, but instead treats it as something to be thought of with an uncomfortable sense of guilt and embarrassment. There is little imagination in the language. There is none of the symbolism of the folk blues. The effect depends on the double meaning; so any imaginative imagery is avoided, and there is not even the directness of an expressed pleasure in the physical sensations described, since what is happening, as it always turns out, isn't sexual.

Often the recordings were done by intelligent and skilled blues artists, but they could bring little to them except their musical sensitivity. Most of the performances that still have any interest have a musical, rather than a poetic,

strength. Sometimes the songs were
even done as duets, with a man and
woman taking alternate verses, but the
result was usually even more dis-
couraging than the records by one
singer, since the skills of two singers
were being wasted on nearly meaningless and often degrading material.
Usually the meaning turned on something that was generally familiar. There
were "Big Truck" or "Big Trunk" blues,
with the man trying to get a "trunk"
into the woman's "closet" or a "truck"
into her "garage." Generally the trunk
is too big and there is considerable
"pushing and squeezing . . ." before
they get it in. There were blues about
dentists, with the usual idea that the
girl should open wide because ". . . it
isn't going to hurt a bit." Some of the
women singers did blues about their
"Handy Man" or their "Kitchen Man,"
usually with a verse that explained that
they loved their handy man or their
kitchen man for his various skills and
they described exactly what he could
do. It is the same use of double meaning
and the singing usually had a leering
style to it that added to the general
effect of cheap vulgarity. Sometimes a
phrase was borrowed from the folk
idiom, but generally there was little
more than a string of clichés. Usually
a handy man was described as being

able to "haul ashes," a folk expression for being able to make love, but his other skills usually were only vaguely related to an open expression of sexuality. A typical blues was something like Sarah Martin's "Kitchen Man." She describes a Madam Buck who has a kitchen man who is leaving her. The woman says that she loves his "turnip tops," his "hash," his "cabbage"; that she can't do without him because. ". . . that boy can open clams," and swears that ". . . No one else is going to touch my hams." By the time she gets to the references to more varied sexual techniques, "anytime he wants to eat he can use my sugar bowl," even she is beginning to sound a little tired of it. The attitude it expresses is the self-conscious sense of shame of the white society that is unable to listen to a song which openly enjoys physical love. Sarah was more or less forced to use material of this kind as her career faded, but she could still sing exultantly, in another blues,

Don't you turn your back on me,
'Cause it ain't never been your shoulder
blades that I wanted to see.
When a lady's speaking don't you
know your place?
How can I get results if I can't see your
face?

Although there is occasionally some
difficulty in understanding the sexual
imagery of the blues there is little use
of the double meaning. The poetic language is honest and direct. One of the
most common expressions used in the
rural blues to describe a lover is "easy
rider," an affectionate reference to the
physical relationship. Sometimes, however, an expression will have several
meanings, and it will change from blues
to blues. A popular phrase, "tight like
that," is used as a sexual term, referring, of course, to the physical union,
or as a description of difficulties or hard
times. As a sexual expression it is usually exuberant, and it is often used in
some of the faster blues for dancing.
The chorus is a shouted,

It's tight like that, yes, yes,
It's tight like that, yes, yes,
Hear me talking to you,
Yes, it's tight like that.

Sometimes instead of "yes, yes" the
singer uses a variation of "beedle um
bum," a meaningless term to fill out the
rhythm of the line.

It's tight like that, beedle um bum,

and many versions of the song were
called "Beedle Um Bum."

Sometimes the verses are specifically
sexual,

Two times three is six,
Three times three is nine,
You give me some of yours,
And I'll give you some of mine.
   'Cause it's tight like that, yes, yes,
   'Cause it's tight like that, yes, yes,
   Hear me talkin' to you,
   Yes, it's tight like that.

Say I got a key,
Shines like gold,
All the women tell me
It satisfies their soul,
      'Cause it's tight like that . . .

Daddy, you could have
Most anything I got,
Because you know
I like you a lot.
      Oh, it's tight like that . . .

Don't get angry,
Don't be sad,
Goin' to give you something
That you never had,
      Oh, it's tight like that . . .

Early in the morning,
Break of day,
I heard a man and his woman,
Yes, I heard him say,
      Oh, it's tight like that . . .

while other verses, in the same per-
formance, would use the phrase in its
other meaning, of a difficult or unpleas-
ant situation.

Going away, mama,
Won't be back 'til fall.
Times don't get better
Won't be back at all
    It's tight like that . . .

Now listen, woman,
What have you done?
You made me love you
Now your man done come,
    It's tight like that . . .

A well-known verse also expresses another sexual attitude, that men who are
considerate are more desirable to the
women.

I ain't good looking,
And I don't dress fine,
But the women all love me,
Say I take my time,
    Oh, it's tight like that . . .

In his blues, "My Wife Drove Me
From My Door," Charlie Lincoln took
the same attitude, and it is also used by
a number of other singers.

Some men don't like me because they
    says I speaks my mind,

> *I know the mens don't like me because*
> *they says I speaks my mind,*
> *But the women crazy about me, 'cause*
> *they say I takes my time.*

Trixie Smith, in describing why she loved her man, sang,

> *My daddy likes it slow, in the mornings,*
> *My daddy likes it slow.*

The directness of a phrase like "it's tight like that," is a reflection of sexual attitudes that are neither sentimental and misleading, as in American popular song, or ashamed and uncomfortable, as in the party records. With this directness there is a wide use of a number of sexual images in a highly figurative poetic language. One of the best-known images is "jelly roll," or, as it is often used, simply "jelly." Its meaning is very specific,

> *She's got a sweet jelly, my woman's*
> *got a sweet jelly roll.*
> *Yes, she's got a sweet jelly, my*
> *woman's got a sweet jelly roll.*
> *It takes her jelly to satisfy my soul.*

but like the imagery of other folk poetry its meanings have an elusive wildness. Even in its most basic intent, a term to describe the vagina, it has al-

ready expressed an attitude toward sex.
It is the sweetness of jelly roll that is
implied in the term, and from this is
inferred the sweetness of the sexual embrace. A singer is thinking of the sweetness as he uses the term to describe
himself.

I got good jelly, I like to give it away.
I got good jelly, I like to give it away.
My sweet woman likes to have it every
day.

The image is heightened as another
singer remembers that jelly roll is
baked.

My woman sure knows how to bake
good jelly roll.
My woman sure knows how to bake
good jelly roll.
She bakes so much it always makes
me full.

It is only another step in the same
imaginative direction to the idea of
"baking jelly roll" as an expression
meaning the sexual embrace, and in an
extravagantly imaginative flight Lonnie
Johnson sang,

She said, Mr. Jelly Roll Baker, let me be
your slave.

When Gabriel blows his trumpet then
    I'll rise from my grave,
For some of your good jelly roll,
Yes, I love your jelly roll,
It's good for the sick, yes,
And it's good for the old . . .

She said, Can I put an order in, for two
    weeks ahead?
I'd rather have your jelly roll than my
    home-cooked bread.
I love your jelly roll,
I love your good jelly roll.

The phrase "home-cooked bread" refers to the love-making of the woman's husband, and bread, cake, biscuits, as well as nearly every kind of pastry, have become sexual terms with some of the derivations as jelly roll. In another blues it is the jelly which has become the sexual image.

You've got to whip it to a jelly.
You've got to stir it in a bowl.
You've got to whip it to a jelly
If you want good jelly roll.

Sometimes the imagery becomes so elaborate that it is difficult to trace the implications of every phrase. In his "Baker Shop Blues" Blind Lemon Jefferson has woven an elaborate texture of sexual and social implications.

I was standing front of the bakery shop
    and I was feeling low down in
    my mind.
Standing front of the bakery shop I was
    feeling low down in my mind.
Feeling hungry as could be, looking at
    those cakes so fine.

Woman in the bakery shop shouted,
    "Papa, don't look so sad."
Woman in the bakery shop shouted,
    "Papa, don't you look so sad,
Come and try some of my cake and
    you won't feel so bad."

"Sweet rolls in the window, honey, light
    bread's getting cold.
Sweet rolls in the window, honey, light
    bread's getting cold."
I wanted to buy me some cakes, but I
    had shot some dice and lost my
    roll.

I'm crazy about my light bread and my
    pigmeat on the side.
I say I'm crazy about my light bread
    and my pigmeat on the side.
But if I taste your jelly roll I be satisfied.

I want to know if your jelly roll's fresh,
    if your jelly roll's stale.
Well, I want to know if your jelly roll's
    fresh, if your jelly roll's stale.

> I'm going to haul off and buy me some
> if I have to break it loose in jail.
> It's hard to be broke, so hungry you're
> 'bout to drop.
> It's hard to be broke, so hungry you're
> 'bout to drop.
> But if I don't break through I'll fall dead
> in front of this bakery shop.

Although the meaning of "jelly roll" has been broadened until the term has the widest sexual implications the expressions referring to the penis are more restricted. One of the most direct of the erotic blues is Blind Lemon Jefferson's "Black Snake Moan," which uses the common Texas symbolism of the black snake as first recorded by a young girl from outside of Dallas, Victoria Spivey.

> Hey—ain't got no mama now.
> Hey—ain't got no mama now.
> She told me late last night, you don't
> need no mama no how.

As Lemon is singing he is already feeling the frustration of desire.

> Um—um, black snake crawling in my
> room.
> Um—um, black snake crawling in my
> room.

Yes, some pretty mama better get this
   black snake soon.

Uum—what's the matter now?
Uum—what's the matter now?
Tell me what's the matter, baby? "I
   don't like no black snake
   nohow."

He has gotten a girl to visit him, but
she refuses to lie with him. She answers
his questioning, "Tell me what's the
matter, baby?" with her petulant, "I
don't like no black snake nohow."

Well, I wonder where this black snake's
   gone.
I wonder where this black snake's gone.
Lord, that black snake, mama, done run
   my mama home.

The "sweet potato" usually has the
same intent as the "black snake" in its
erotic meanings. As Texas Alexander
used in a complaint about women,

I got a sweet potato and it's nice and
   hot.
I got a sweet potato and it's nice and
   hot.
Before I give it away I'll let it rot.

The image is often extended to include the embrace itself,

My good woman had a sweet potato
in her hand.
My good woman had a sweet potato
in her hand.
If you want good potato you can bake
it in my pan.

and "digging potatoes" becomes a term
for intercourse. Ida Cox sang,

If he didn't like my potatoes, why did
he dig so deep?
If he didn't like my potatoes, why did
he dig so deep?
In his mama's potato patch five and ten
times a week?

The "lemon" is also used in the same
sense as the black snake and the sweet
potato, but it is sometimes interpreted
as either masculine or feminine. As the
image was used by One-String, an itin-
erant musician playing a home-made
one string instrument who was recorded by Frederick Usher Jr. in an alley in
the Los Angeles skid row area, it was
masculine.

Well, you squeezed my lemon, baby,
and you started my juice to run,
Well, you squeezed my lemon, baby,
and you started my juice to run.

But as it was sung by the Brownsville,

Tennessee, singer, Charlie Pickett, it
was feminine.

I say makes no difference, baby,
What your daddy don't 'low.
Let me squeeze your lemon, mama,
I mean anyhow,
*   I said please let me squeeze your*
*   lemon,*
*   While I'm in your lonesome town.*
*   Now let me squeeze your lemon,*
*   baby,*
*   Until my love comes down.*

Often the imagery was taken from
the life in the rural areas. The woman
becomes the "milk cow."

If you see my milk cow, won't you send
*   her home.*
If you see my milk cow, won't you
*   please send her home.*
I ain't had no milk since she been gone.

In his "Milk Cow's Calf Blues," Robert
Johnson elaborated on the image, as
Blind Lemon Jefferson had done in his
"Baker Shop Blues," extending it until
the meaning becomes difficult to inter-
pret.

Tell me, milk cow, what on earth is
*   wrong with you.*

*Uumh, milk cow, what on earth is wrong
    with you.*
*Now you have a little milk calf and
    your milk is turning blue.*

*Now your calf is hungry, I believe he
    needs to suck.*
*And now your calf is hungry, I believe
    he needs to suck.*
*But your milk is turning blue, I believe
    he's out of luck.*

*I feel like milking,
    And my milk won't come,
    I feel like chewing it,
    And my milk won't turn,*
*I'm crying please, please don't do me
    wrong.*
*If you see my milk cow, baby, now,
    please drive her home.*

*My milk cow been rambling for miles
    around.*
*My milk cow been rambling for miles
    around.*
*She must have settled for some man's
    bull cow in the same town . . .*

Sometimes, in the rural imagery, the
man is described as a "groundhog," or
as a "rooting groundhog." As Little Son
Jackson used it, it meant a man who
was trying to take advantage of other
men's wives.

There's a groundhog rooting, rooting in
      the next door yard.
Ain't nothing can stop him, unless the
      ground gets real hard.

If I catch a hog in my yard just before
      day,
I'm going to get my double-barrelled
      shotgun and drive that hog
      away.

Well, there's a groundhog for
      tomorrow, for the next day, too.
Well, there's a groundhog 'cross the
      country you don't know.

Yes, there's a groundhog in your yard,
Ain't nothing can stop him, 'less that
      ground's real hard.

There is even a highly figurative language describing the movements of the
embrace in terms of things done in the
kitchen. Rolling biscuits becomes for
One-String,

Well, I can roll my belly like your
      mama roll her dough,
Say the reason I know it 'cause my
      good gal she told me so.

and for Cat-Iron,

Don't your house look lonesome, your
      biscuit roller done gone.

> Don't your house look lonesome, when
>> your biscuit roller done gone.
> Don't your house look lonesome, find
>> your baby gone.

Coffee grinding becomes a sexual image with the same meaning.

> I got a coffee-grinder, got the best one I
>> could find.
> Got me a coffee-grinder, got me the best
>> one I could find.
> So he could grind my coffee with his
>> special grind.

Even the movements of a child's toy, the yo-yo, suggests the embrace. As Texas Alexander sang,

> When you get to yo-yoing you jumps it
>> up and down,
> When you get to yo-yoing you jumps it
>> up and down,
> But when you learns how to yo-yo you
>> turn it 'round and 'round.

In the early 1950's Piano Red had a very successful recording, with the exuberant chorus, "You got the right string, baby, but the wrong yo-yo."

With the imagery of the farm and the kitchen there is a rich area of imagery which has grown out of newer mechanical objects. There are many blues which use the automobile as an erotic symbol. Robert Johnson's "Terraplane Blues," with its elaborate symbolism centered on the Terraplane, a car produced by Hudson Motors, was commercially his most successful recording.

When I feel so lonesome, you hear me
    when I moan.
When I feel so lonesome, you hear me
    when I moan.
Who's been driving my terraplane for
    you, babe, since I been gone.

Since the woman won't respond to his lovemaking he decides that she's been with somebody else, warning her, as an afterthought, that he has another girl in Arkansas.

I said I flashed your lights, mama, your
    horn won't even blow.
I even flashed the lights, mama, this
    horn won't even blow.
There's a short in this connection way
    down below.

I'm going to hoist your hood, mama, I'm
    bound to check your oil.
I'm going to hoist your hood, mama, I'm
    bound to check your oil.

> I got a woman that I'm loving 'way
> down in Arkansas.

He complains again that she must have been with somebody else; then tells people to get out of his way because he's driving the terraplane at ". . . a cold one hundred." In a final verse he tells her that he intends to keep on making love to her until she responds to him.

Now you know the car ain't even
buzzing,
Their generator won't get their spark,
All under bad condition,
You got to have these batteries charged,
I'm crying please, please don't do me
wrong,
Who's been driving my terraplane now,
since I been gone.

Mister highway man, please don't block
the road,
Mister highway man, please don't block
the road,
'Cause she's hitting a cold one hundred,
and I'm booked and I got to go.

I'm going to get deep down in this
connection, keep on tangling
with your wires,
I'm going to get deep down in this
connection, keep on tangling
with your wires,

And when I mash down on your starter,
then your spark plug will give
me fire.

There are so many blues using the
automobile that it is difficult to listen to
a blues verse which mentions anything
that relates to cars or driving without
finding a sexual implication. There are,
however, some singers who have sung
about automobiles without intending
anything beyond the literal meaning of
the verse. In his "T-Model Ford Blues"
Sleepy John Estes sang,

Well, the T-Model Ford I say is the poor
man's friend.
Well, the T-Model Ford I say is the poor
man's friend.
Well, well, it will help you out when
your money's thin.

Well, one thing about a T-Model, you
don't have to shift no gears.
Well, one thing about a T-Model, you
don't have to shift no gears.
Well, well, just let down your brake and
feed the gas and the stuff is
here . . .

Well, well, somebody they done stole
wine out on the road.
Well, well, somebody they done stole
wine out on the road.

Well, just find somebody got a T-Model Ford.

His song, however, is more remarkable for being literal than it would be for using as sexual imagery. The "chauffeur" is almost invariably an erotic symbol. One-String uses it in a song that tries to soften its intent with a literal ending to the verse, but that still remains stubbornly physical.

Come on and be my chauffeur,
Come on and be my chauffeur,
I want you to drive me,
I want you to drive me,
   downtown.

I don't want him,
I don't want him,
To be riding these girls,
To be riding these girls,
   around.

I'm going to let him,
I'm going to let him,
Ride me around,
Ride me around,
   this world.

If he'll be my little boy
I will be his little girl.

Blind Lemon Jefferson was able to turn an oil well into a symbol of physical

love in a blues that even includes a
reference to the innocence of the girl
he's trying to seduce.

Ain't nothing, mama, don't get scared
    at all.
It ain't nothing, mama, don't get scared
    at all.
It's a long distance well, and it's
    running all its oil.

It ain't nothing to hurt you, it ain't
    nothing bad.
Ain't nothing to hurt you, honey, it ain't
    nothing bad.
It's the first oil well that you ever had.

I'm a long-distance driller, wildcat the
    country soon.
I'm a long-distance driller, wildcat the
    country soon.
But I done wildcatting, if I bring in this
    well for you.

He is promising her that if she gives
in to him he'll stop seeing other women.
He goes on to assure her that she'll get
some pleasure from his drilling.

I'm a mean oil well driller, been a
    driller since I been a man,
I'm a mean oil well driller, been a
    driller since I been a man,

> *And I don't stop drilling 'til I strikes that*
> *real fine sand . . .*

One of the most expressive of the erotic images in the blues is the stinging bee, the "stingaree." Just as "jelly roll" suggests the sweetness and the pleasure in sexual experience, the bee suggests the essential innocence. The bee, moving from flower to flower, erratically clumsy, leaving the flower with its beauty unharmed, is a touching symbol for a freely acknowledged sexuality. A singer of the 1930's, Bo Carter, used the imagery of physical love in many of his blues, and his first recording took the bumble bee as its image, boasting,

> *Hey, I'm old bumble bee, a stinger just*
> *long as my arm.*
> *I'm an old bumble bee, a stinger just*
> *long as my arm.*
> *I sting the good-looking women*
> *everywhere I goes along.*

> *As I fly 'round, now, I makes a beautiful*
> *song,*
> *As I fly 'round, now, I makes a beautiful*
> *song,*
> *And everywhere I sting a good-looking*
> *woman, say, I'll sure win me a*
> *home.*

> *Now I'm an old bumble bee,*

Just dropped in your town,
And ain't none of these women
Turn this old bumble bee down.

They cryin', come here, bumble bee,
*   you know your stuff.*
And your stinger, old bumble bee, your
*   stinger just long enough.*

Then when I get to stinging, now I sting
*   just like I should,*
Then when I get to stinging, now I sting
*   just like I should,*
And they crying, old bumble bee, you
*   know it hurts so good.*

8

There is little social protest in the blues. There is often a note of anger and frustration; sometimes the poverty and the rootlessness in which the singer has lived his life is evident in a word or a phrase, but there is little open protest at the social conditions under which a Negro in the United States is forced to live. There is complaint, but protest has been stifled. Slavery, and the period of semislavery that followed the Civil War, was a period of helpless bewilderment for the Negroes who found themselves swept into it. Their tribal beliefs were useless, and they were deprived of the education that might have given them some understanding of the social situation around them. When education finally did come they found that there was still almost no encouragement for them to enter fully into American life. The young Negro, whatever his ambitions or social attitudes, is driven into an unwilling acceptance of what is little more than a semicitizenship. If he is unable to accept it he has little choice except to either leave the country or to

become a social rebel and express his
frustrations in a brief burst of violence.
Much of the fear that the southerner has
for the Negro is his awareness of the
brutality of his treatment of the Negro
and the realization that in a moment the
smoldering animosities could flare up
into an open rage.

It is almost impossible for the white
American to realize how tightly he has
united against his black fellow citizens.
The oppressive weight of prejudice is
so constricting that it is not surprising to
find little protest in the blues. It is surprising to find even an indirect protest.
The white Americans who think of
themselves as liberals are often impa-
tient with what they feel to be the fail-
ure of the black men and women that
they meet to either be more militant in
their demands for equality or to respond to a lessening of the pressure.
They have, to some extent, overcome
much of their own prejudice, but they
forget that the Negro still faces a hostile
wall of hate and distrust. If a black man
or woman is able to get an adequate
education there is still little chance that
there will be any kind of employment
opportunity. If there is a job that pays
well there is still the difficulty of finding
a home. Even if a Negro has achieved
some measure of success he is still re-

stricted in his choice of hotels, restaurants, neighborhoods, friends, and, in many areas, in his right to vote and his legal rights as a citizen. For the blues singer, at the lowest level of society, the situation is so intolerable that if he even thought about it for a period of time he would be destroyed as an individual. In the rural South, where most of the singers still live, every Negro is a marked man. If he protests, his job, his home, his family, and even his life, are at the mercy of his white neighbors, whose attempts to blind themselves to the situation with a meaningless paternal charity have only taken them closer and closer to the violence they have feared for so many years.

Even singers who have had considerable success have found it difficult to develop a social attitude in their blues. Big Bill and Josh White both sang several blues which expressed their anger at the situation, but these came in their later years, when they were appearing before sympathetic audiences, often in Europe. Sometimes at a party a southern singer will begin drinking and his voice will take on an edge of anger, but his blues are still the personal expression of his loves and travels and disappointments. If he does become more general he will probably sing one of the two or three verses that are so widely

known in the South that there will be no
trouble.

The nigger and the white man
Playing Seven up,
The nigger win the pot,
But he's afraid to pick it up.

An old folk song is also well known, the
references changed to suit the singer's
own social background.

The white man he rides in a great big
car,
The brownskin man does the same,
The black man he rides around in a
T-Model Ford,
But he gets there just the same.

As Son House sang, at the persistent
request of a field collector for the folk
song archives of the Library of Con-
gress,

Down South when you do anything
that's wrong,
Down South when you do anything
that's wrong,
Down South when you do anything
that's wrong,
They'll sure put you down on the
country farm.

Put you down under a man called
Captain Jack.

> Put you under a man called Captain
> Jack.
> Put you under a man they call Captain
> Jack.
> He'll sure write his name up and down
> your back.

> Put you down in a ditch with a great big
> spade.
> Put you down in a ditch with a great big
> spade.
> Put you down in a ditch with a great big
> spade.
> Wish to God you hadn't ever been
> made.

In the blues, however, can be seen
some of the attitudes which the social
pressure has built up in the Negro. It is
not social protest, or even complaint,
but in its implications there is reflected
some of the difficulty of the continual
adjustment to the insult and the injustice of the color line. There is a continual concern in some blues with the
varying shades of skin color. Since it
was the blackness of the skin that
marked the Negro it became associated
with evil. One-String sang,

> Well, that jet black woman like to scare
> my mule to death.
> That jet black woman like to scare my
> mule to death.

*If I had not had that special, man, I
would have run myself.*

"Special" is a term for revolver. Cat-
Iron repeated a commonly held notion
that the black woman is a sorceress.

*I don't want no black woman, fryin' no
meat for me.*
*I don't want no black woman, fryin' no
meat for me.*

*For she studies evil, she's liable to
poison me.*

Among the woman singers there was
often a concern with the relationship between the color of their man's skin and
his ideas of fidelity. Since a man with
light skin was closer to social acceptance they often felt that he would be
difficult to keep.

*I don't want no brownskin, he won't do
me no good.*
*I don't want no brownskin, he won't do
me no good.*
*He'll fool 'round with other women,
won't come home when he
should.*

They felt that a man with darker skin
would be more grateful for their attention.

> *Going to find me a black man*
> *somewhere in this town.*
> *Going to find me a black man*
> *somewhere in this town.*
> *Black man will stay by you when your*
> *brownskin throws you down.*

But the concern with skin color is a minor strain in the blues. Related to it is the difficulty which Negroes from rural areas had adjusting to the life of the cities both in the North and South. Sophistication, like a light skin color, represents a step away from the lowest level of society. Rabbit Brown, a street entertainer in New Orleans, sang,

> *'Cause I was born in the country she*
> *thinks I'm easy to rule.*
> *'Cause I was born in the country she*
> *thinks I'm easy to rule.*
> *She tried to hitch me to a wagon she*
> *tried to drive me like a mule.*

Furry Lewis had the same comment.

> *When I had my money it was hello*
> *sugar pie.*
> *When I had my money it was hello*
> *sugar pie.*
> *Now I done got broke it's so long*
> *country guy.*

The most complete break that someone

could make with the life in the South
was to move to a northern city, but it
was a frightening trip for a man or a
woman who had little social experience
and knew little about life outside the
county where they had been born and
raised. They found themselves without
jobs, sometimes without even anyone to
help them, usually living in a crowded
tenement in a crumbling slum area. It
was difficult to stick it out during the
first months. During the depression
years thousands were driven back to
the South. Often in the North they
found themselves ridiculed by people
who had arrived a year or so earlier,
and had already acquired some knowl-
edge of the city life. In a reference to
the yearly payments which a share-
cropper was used to receiving, Jazz
Gillum sang,

You want a whole lot of credit
To pay off once a year,
But you owe the salary you make
For just liquor and beer.
You better go back to the country,
'Way back out in the woods.
I'm tired of hearin' you hollerin' City
       Lights ain't no good . . .

They found, too, that the life was still
difficult.

> *I would stay up North, but nothing here
> that I can do,*
> *I would stay up North, but nothing here
> that I can do.*
> *Just stand around the corner and sing
> my lonesome blues.*

The women found that they couldn't handle the city men. Ida Cox complained,

> *When I was down South I wouldn't take
> no one's advice.*
> *When I was down South I wouldn't take
> no one's advice.*
> *But I won't let that same bee sting me
> twice.*

> *I don't want no northern yellow, no
> northern black or brown.*
> *I don't want no northern yellow, no
> northern black or brown.*
> *Southern men will stick by you when
> the northern men can't be found.*

Sometimes alcohol was used as an escape from the situation. Furry Lewis tried to reason with his woman.

> *Now you know you didn't want me
> when you laid down across my
> bed,*
> *Drinking your white lightning and
> talking all out of your head.*

You know you didn't want me when
*   you laid down across my bed.*
Drinking your white lightning and
*   talking all out of your head.*

J. D. Short referred to wine, the common
drink with impoverished alcoholics,
white and black.

Knees got the rickets, head got to
*   rolling.*
Keep on drinking, sweet Lucy, life won't
*   last me long.*
I drink so much wine,
Yes, so much wine.

Black Ace warned his woman that if
she didn't stop drinking she'd find "the
deal gone down," meaning that their
relationship would be over.

You know you spent all your money for
*   Seagram "Seven Crown."*
You know you spent all your money for
*   Seagram "Seven Crown."*
Now if you ever gets sober, mama, you
*   will find that the deal's gone*
*   down.*

For many of the singers, footloose
wanderers at the edges of society,
prison is a harsh reality. In the smaller
towns of the South any unfamiliar Negro could be picked up for vagrancy.

There was a continual need for labor on the roads and for city maintenance; so local sheriffs had no hesitation in making arrests. Behind the police brutality and intimidation there was also the fear of the Negro, and the helplessness of the lone black man as he tried to stand up against the corruption and the dishonesty of southern "law enforcement" was one of the most demoralizing aspects of his situation. It was an unwritten law in many areas that a Negro who had a white man behind him could commit almost any crime against another Negro without fear of the law. The most serious crime was to be without a white man willing to talk to the sheriff and the judge. Sleepy John Estes referred to this in his "Jailhouse Blues."

Now, I was sitting in jail with my eyes
    all full of tears.
Now, I was sitting in jail with my eyes
    all full of tears.
You know I'm glad I didn't get lifetime,
    boys, that I 'scaped the 'lectric
    chair.

Now, I consulted lawyers, and I know
    darn well I was wrong.
Now, I consulted lawyers, and I know
    darn well I was wrong.

You know I could not get a white man
> in Brownsville, yes, to even go
> my bond.

In 1959 Dr. Harry Oster of Louisiana
State University recorded prisoners in
the penitentiary at Angola, Louisiana,
and in their blues was a desolate cry of
defeat, of anger, and of despair. They
were men for whom time had become
only a monotonous succession of days
without meaning or hope. Guitar Welch
sang,

I'm gonna shake hands with my
> partner, I'm gonna ask him how
> come he here,
I'm gonna shake hands with my
> partner, I'm gonna ask him how
> come he here.
You know I had a wreck in my family,
> they're gonna send me to the old
> electric chair.

Wonder why they electrocute a man at
> the one o'clock hour at night?
Wonder why they electrocute a man,
> baby, Lord, at the one o'clock
> hour at night?
The current much stronger, people turn
> out all the light . . .

Hogman Maxey felt his weariness and
pain at the end of the long prison day.

Oh, black night fallin', my pains comin'
    down again.
Oh, black night fallin', my pains comin'
    down again.
Oh, I feel so lonesome, oh I ain't got no
    friend.

Oh, oh, just another pain, oh Lord, it
    hurts so bad.
Mm, just another pain, oh Lord, oh it
    hurts so bad.
Lord, I feel so lonesome, baby, lost the
    best friend I ever had.

Oh, sheets and pillow cases torn all to
    pieces, baby, bloodstain all over
    the wall.
Mm, sheets and pillows torn all to
    pieces, baby, and bloodstain all
    on the wall.
Oh, Lord, I wasn't aiming when I left,
    baby, and the telephone wasn't
    in the hall . . .

For Robert Pete Williams the blues
were an expression of his feeling at the
injustice that had been done to him.

Some got six months, some got a solid
    year,
But me and my buddy, we got life time
    here.
Some got six months, some got a solid
    year,

But me and my buddy, we got life time
    here.

Six months, oh baby, let me go to bed.
I've drunk white lightning, gone to my
    head.
It gone to my head.

I've got so much of time, darling,
It worryin' me, oh babe.
You know this time killin' me,
But I just can't help it, darling, I just got
    to roll.

You know that old judge must been
    mad.
Yeh, that old judge must been mad,
    darling.
When he gave me my sentence he
    throwed the book at me.

First time in trouble I done get no fair
    trial at all, oh Lord.
Seem like to me, baby, they locked the
    poor boy in jail.

When there is complaint in the blues
it usually is personal, even if it concerns the drudgery of the laboring jobs
that are often the best a Negro can hope
to get.

I do more work, Lord, than a pair of
    twins.

I do more work, Lord, than a pair of
*   twins.*
My body's aching from my head down
*   to my shins.*

Bessie Smith complained of the wash-woman's life.

Sorry I do washing just to make my
*   livelihood.*
Sorry I do washing just to make my
*   livelihood.*
Oh the washwoman's life it ain't a bit
*   of good.*

Rather be a scullion, cooking in some
*   white folks' yard.*
Rather be a scullion, cooking in some
*   white folks' yard.*
I could eat up plenty, wouldn't have to
*   work so hard.*

But even the life of a cook was difficult. For Clara Smith it meant the scorn of other women,

Women talk about me, they lies on me,
*   call me out of my name.*
They talk about me, lies on me, call me
*   out of my name.*
All their men come to see me just the
*   same.*

I'm just a workin' gal, oh workin' gal,

kitchen mechanic is what they
say,
I'm just a workin' gal, oh workin' gal,
kitchen mechanic is what they
say,
But I'll have an honest dollar on that
rainy day . . .

Sometimes the complaint was more
general, at the W. P. A., or at unemployment. In nearly all of these blues,
however, the complaint is still personal,
or the larger social theme is only used
to introduce one of the common blues
attitudes. A W. P. A. blues will often
have as little real social consciousness
as a blues of infidelity. The first verse
may mention the subject,

W. P. A. done tore my baby's
playhouse down.
W. P. A. done tore my baby's
playhouse down.
Done took my baby, she's nowhere
around.

but the verses that follow usually return
to a standard blues pattern.

I wonder where's my baby, I wonder
where could she be,
I wonder where's my baby, I wonder
where could she be,

> She's gone somewheres, she's gone
>   and left poor me.

In 1930 Bo Carter sang of the first
months of the depression, but three of
the six verses are concerned with problems that this has raised between men
and women, and one concerns his own
sexual relationships. The other two di-
rectly mention the difficulties of the
period, but each verse ends with a refrain insisting that Carter isn't going to
worry about it.

> These times and days, I can't
>   understand.
> Just 'cause times is hard the women
>   want to change men.
> 'Cause times is hard, but I don't worry.
> I got the whole world in my hand.

> These times and days worried
>   everybody's mind.
> You often find men who haven't got a
>   dime.
> 'Cause times is hard, but I don't worry.
> I got the whole world in my hand.

> I'm tellin' you the truth, as the good
>   Lord who's above,
> The women all 'stand, can't live off of
>   love.
> 'Cause times is hard, but I don't worry.
> I got the whole world in my hand.

Let me tell you one thing, woman,
      surely true,
That as you change men you won't
      have no more.
'Cause times is hard, but I don't worry.
I got the whole world in my hand.

The clothes in rags, no shoes on my
      feet,
But that ain't the main question, they
      want something to eat.
'Cause times is hard, but I don't worry.
I got the whole world in my hand.

It was late last night, hear my baby
      cry,
You know it's all night long, daddy,
      please take your time.
'Cause times is hard, but I don't worry.
You got the whole world in your hand.

The momentary reference to the social
conditions is immediately vivid, but it
is almost lost in the emotional emphasis of the blues. There are a few singers
who try to deal with social problems,
but even in their own compositions it is
still love, and its pain and disappointment, that dominate the blues. One of
the few songs which makes a funda-
mental attack on the American system
is, ironically, an attack on the economic
system rather than on the social justice. Bessie Smith would have found it

difficult to record a song that dealt with
racial intolerance, but she was able to
sing a blues that is openly socialistic.

Mr. Rich Man, Mr. Rich Man, open up
    your heart and mind.
Mr. Rich Man, Mr. Rich Man, open up
    your heart and mind.
Give the poor man a chance, help stop
    these hard, hard times.

While you living in your mansion you
    don't know what hard times
    means.
While you living in your mansion you
    don't know what hard times
    means.
Poor working man's wife is starving
    while your wife is living like a
    queen.

Please listen to my pleading, 'cause I
    can't stand these hard times
    long.
Oh, listen to my pleading, can't stand
    these hard times long.
They'll make an honest man to think
    that you know is wrong.

If all men thought the better a man
    would start again today.
If all men thought the better a man
    would start again today.

He would do anything you ask him in
the name of the U. S. A.

When the war is over all men must live
the same as you.
And the war is over all men must live
the same as you.
If it wasn't for the poor man, Mr. Rich
Man, what would you do?

The blues, however, has lost little by
its lack of concern with social protest
and comment. The greatness of poetry
is its power to express the individual
emotion, the personal response to the
reality of experience. It is the cry of
pain, the shout of joy, the whisper of
love, and the murmur of despair at
separation and death. Even in the poor-
est poetry it is the momentary emotion
which is usually the poet's concern,
rather than the opinions and details of
social commentary. As Archibald Mac-
Leish expressed it,

"The things of the poet are done to a
man alone . . ."

In the greatest blues there is often a
reflection of the social restrictions which
encircle the singer, but in the situation
he is able to find the things ". . . done
to a man alone . . ." In his "Crossroads Blues" Robert Johnson cries out

to someone to save him as he stands at
a crossroad trying to get a ride. There
is nowhere for him to go. He doesn't
know of any women living nearby. In
desperation he calls to someone passing to tell his friend Willie Brown, another singer from Clarksdale, that he is
". . . sinking down." The reason for
his desperation is that he is in a Mississippi county that jails any Negro
found on the roads after dark. But instead of an explanation he only cries
out in his fear, and it is the intensity of
his cry that gives his blues its poetic
strength.

I went to the crossroads, fell down on
    my knees.
I went to the crossroads, fell down on
    my knees.
I asked the Lord above, have mercy,
    save poor Bob if you please.

Uumh, standing at the crossroads I tried
    to flag a ride.
Standing at the crossroads I tried to flag
    a ride.
Ain't nobody seem to know me,
    everybody pass me by.

And the sun going down, boys, dark
    gone catch me here.
Uumh, oh dark gone catch me here.

*I haven't got no loving sweet woman,
    that love will be near.*

*You can run, you can run, tell my friend
    poor Willie Brown,*
*You can run, tell my friend poor Willie
    Brown,*
*Lord, that I'm standing at the
    crossroads, babe, I believe I'm
    sinking down.*

There will be social change, too, in
the United States, and if the blues simply mirrored the protest of the moment
they would finally have little more than
an historical interest, like the songs of
the suffragettes or the Grange move-
ment. Instead, as the Negro in America
has struggled to find a life on the other
side of the racial line he has turned to
the blues as the expression of his personal and immediate experience, and
in their directness and in their concern
with what the singers call the " . . .
true feeling" the blues express a larger
human reality. In the honesty of their
emotion is an insistent reminder that on
either side of the racial line live only
other men and women, who find the
same moments of pain and joy in the
experience of life.

A SELECTED BIBLIOGRAPHY

Cash, W. J., *The Mind of the South*. New York:
    A. A. Knopf, 1941.
Charters, Samuel B., *The Country Blues*. New York:
    Rinehart, 1959.
Dollard, John, *Caste And Class In A Southern Town*.
    New Haven: Yale Univ. Press, 1937.
Odum, Howard W., and Johnson, Guy B.,
    Negro Workaday Songs. Chapel Hill: The
    Univ. of North Carolina Press, 1926.
Oliver, Paul, *Blues Fell This Morning*, London:
    Cassell, 1960.
Stampp, Kenneth, *The Peculiar Institution*, New York:
    A. A. Knopf, 1956.